BRASS IN YOUR SCHOOL

Brass in Your School

IAN LAWRENCE

LONDON
OXFORD UNIVERSITY PRESS
NEW YORK   TORONTO
1975

Oxford University Press, Ely House, London W.1
Glasgow New York Toronto Melbourne Wellington
Cape Town Ibadan Nairobi Dar Es Salaam Lusaka Addis Ababa
Delhi Bombay Calcutta Madras Karachi Lahore Dacca
Kuala Lumpur Singapore Hong Kong Tokyo

ISBN 0 19 31 8705 1

© Oxford University Press 1975

Typeset by Preface Ltd., Salisbury
Printed by the Camelot Press Ltd., Southampton

Contents

List of Illustrations

(*reproduced by courtesy of Boosey & Hawkes Ltd.*)

1 Why Brass?

During the past fifteen years the number of young people learning to play brass instruments has greatly increased. The increase, moreover, has been considerably more rapid for brass than for stringed or woodwind instruments. Among the factors which have contributed to this situation are the following: in some respects technical progress, in the early stages at least, seems to be more rapid on brass instruments than on others; the possibilities of playing ensemble music occur very early on in the player's progress; brass instruments are less susceptible to damage than strings or woodwind, and do not have the running costs and problems of replacing strings or reeds; brass players can find a place not only in chamber music and orchestral music, but also in jazz groups, dance bands, wind bands, and Brass Bands with capital Bs; and finally — and very significantly — the repertoire of published music of good quality has grown in step with the demands of players and teachers.

One of the happier developments in musical education in recent times has been the breaking down of barriers between performing groups. No one today would find it in any way strange that a trombone player, for example, should take a vigorous part in many-sided musical activities, moving from a brass band suite to a Venetian canzona, from an improvisation in a jazz group to an improvisation in a piece by Boulez or Berio, from an orchestral overture to a movement for solo trombone and piano. Provided that such a player develops a sense of appropriate styles of performance, he will find that he is able to participate in a great range of worthwhile musical experiences.

Young people often learn to make satisfying sounds on

brass instruments with astonishing speed. Within a year of starting to play, many under-tens are capable of making a real contribution to group music making, and if they are fortunate enough to be allowed to play with older and more experienced players, they often make quite remarkable progress. There was a time when many people supposed brass teaching to be essentially a secondary school activity: it is now generally recognized that as soon as a youngster has grown his second set of teeth (or at least the front ones) he is ready to take on all except the very large instruments. Even the trombone is no trouble if the short-armed player is provided with an arm extension of the sort that used to be associated with the older bass trombones. Of course, children do have a habit of breaking their teeth, but modern techniques in dentistry seem to be capable of providing replacements without too much trouble. The many fine performances that can be heard in the youth divisions of brass band competition bear testimony to the progress that can be made by young players if they are given a proper start at an early stage by good teachers.

Ensemble work for a young quartet of, say, two trumpets, horn, and trombone, provides far fewer problems than does music for a string quartet (for technical reasons), or for a woodwind quartet (for economic reasons, owing to the price of bassoons). Simple parts in the band also provide the younger players with an opportunity to join in the music-making in a way that young brass players will never have available to them in the orchestral repertoire, where they are often confronted either with very exposed passages at climaxes, or a great deal of tension-inducing bar counting.

The brass band has for many years lived a rather isolated existence, partly because of self-constructed barriers, partly because of the prejudices which were fostered in the minds of many professional musicians. Although there are still many obstacles to be overcome in the complete integration of the brass band into the musical community, it needs no apology in today's educational scene, for not only does it provide for many worthwhile musical experiences, but it also has the power to create a unique sense of group awareness among its players.

Among certain people it has become fashionable to discourage children from thinking in competitive terms. Yet there can be little doubt in the minds of teachers who have heard the improvement in playing standards that usually accompany a band's entry into the world of competitions, that this may have a useful part to play in musical development. Too many competitions, on the other hand, are counter-productive, fostering a superficial approach towards musical development. Moreover, music especially written for competitions is often completely devoid of any real musical worth, and is simply constructed to provide problems of a technical nature.

The dance band can give brass players plenty to do, and any music which encourages young players to develop their ability to improvise should have a place in schools. The brass family also is capable of providing plenty of volume, and schools which can provide at least some of the music for their own social occasions and dances may help to re-establish the idea that musicians do not depend entirely upon the wonders of modern electronic amplification.

For players who have mastered the first stages in the development of their technique, the pleasures of playing in orchestral music and in brass chamber music are incalculable. The role of the brass instruments in many orchestral scores is very exciting, and many young players find great satisfaction from playing in a sixty- to eighty-piece orchestra. The brass ensemble, ranging in size from the quartet to the twenty-two-part group of Gabrieli's largest canzona, also provides the developing player with the sort of musical challenges that are found in all branches of chamber music. 'Chamber music' is not perhaps the most appropriate term for the musical repertoire of small brass groups, but at the same time it does emphasize that quality that can be found in the best brass playing, where flexible phrasing and dynamics can play a major part in the building up of a performance.

The development of a satisfying repertoire for young players is one of the principal tasks of the teacher. Today he can be confident that there is no lack of suitable material. There is a great deal of interesting original material published for brass solos (with piano accompaniment) and for brass ensembles. Most of this was written in this century, and like any other body of music, some of it is good and some bad. The good material is certainly worth playing, but it must be investigated, for many of the composers will be unfamiliar to those whose experience of modern music has been confined to the music of Stravinsky, Bartók, and other prominent figures.

The pre-classical repertoire is very extensive indeed, and appears to be keeping editors constantly involved in creating modern playing scores. In the strictest sense, this is not 'authentic' brass music, but the music of the late sixteenth and seventeenth centuries certainly transfers very well to modern instruments. Here we encounter the music of the Venetians, of whom Giovanni Gabrieli is arguably the supreme example; then there are the seventeenth-century English composers, with their exciting rhythmic vitality and harmonic individuality, and the equally fascinating German contemporaries of Schütz. Lastly, there is the brass music of the late baroque, with its brilliant trumpet and intriguing horn parts.

There are also arrangements of classical and romantic works not originally conceived for brass instruments, but often suitably adapted to the needs of brass players. It must be recognized that publications in this category have for many years supplied the basic needs of brass players in schools, and will no doubt continue to do so. Nevertheless, arrangements should be approached with some discrimination, and where authentic pieces of a similar standard exist, should be used only as a second source of supply.

From these three major sources the music teacher can be confident that young players can be supplied with a very large repertoire. However, for the teacher who is interested in making his own arrangements or who has taught his more experienced players the basic procedures of arranging, there opens up an enormous field of possible material. Programmes by professional brass groups now regularly include arrangements of vocal polyphonic music of the renaissance, as well as ingenious realizations of dances originally intended for the virginals or lute. There is no doubt that such music sounds very well on brass instruments, and provides a wealth of subtle rhythmic ideas and intricate textures. It is equally certain that the whole process of making arrangements is of great value in the development of a young musician's skills.

Perhaps the most important point of all, however, is that the school which involves itself in the development of brass playing must not only have the services of good brass teachers, but must also have on the permanent staff someone who, if not a brass player himself, is sympathetic to the problems of brass players, and has a reasonable understanding of the role of brass in school. Without these two ingredients, there is little hope of any real progress being made, however much time or money is devoted to the cause.

2 The Instruments

The instruments that are normally encountered in schools belong to two major categories:

Orchestral brass: B♭ trumpets, F horns, trombones (with or without F attachments), and F tubas.

Band instruments: B♭ and E♭ cornets, flugelhorns, E♭ (tenor) horns, B♭ baritone horns, trombones, B♭ euphoniums, and E♭ and BB♭ basses (tubas).

It is clear that, in the strictest terms, the only instrument that is common to both groups is the trombone. However, in practice, trumpets, cornets, and flugels share the same compass and the same fingering, and — in the schools at least — parts written for one instrument can be played on another. Tuba parts can also be played on whatever instrument is available, although the very large bass tuba cannot, of course, cope with the parts written for the highest compass of the F and E♭ instruments. The teacher who is not familiar with all these instruments must, first of all, get to know the basic information.

The Harmonic Series

All brass instruments depend upon the action of a generator — the player's vibrating lips — combined with a resonator — the air column contained in the tubing of the instrument. Pitch depends upon factors which include the length of the tube and the pattern of vibrations caused by the lips. This pattern determines the frequency of the notes produced and conforms to the harmonic series:

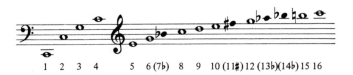

The fundamental (1) cannot be played on some instruments, or by some players. In practice, only the F Horn uses notes above the 8th harmonic with any consistency.

Trombones lengthen the column of air by extending the slide, while other instruments employ valves to add extra lengths of tubing to the main column. e.g.

TRUMPET (*plate 1*)

Modern trumpets are generally built in three sizes: the largest is the B♭ instrument, and this is also by far the most common, and certainly the one most likely to be encountered in schools. The smaller C and D instruments (the latter available with an E♭ connection) are indispensable to the professional orchestral player, but a luxury elsewhere. The trumpet is for most of its length a cylindrical tube, tending to produce a clear edge to its tone.

Written compass:

Sounding (on B♭ instrument):

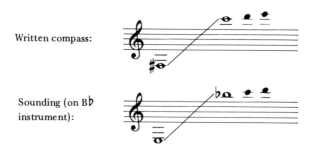

Notes above the sixth harmonic are tiring for the lips, and so passages above written G (G_5) always have an element of danger for young players even though they may be within the 'normal' compass. Notes below middle C (C_4) form the least interesting part of the trumpet's compass, and the lowest notes are more difficult to produce in tune.

CORNET (*plate 2*)

Modern cornets are built in B♭ (with the same compass as the B♭ trumpet) and E♭ (with a compass a fourth higher). They are conical in construction, and tend to produce a 'rounder' tone quality than the trumpet, but this is very much a matter of the player's technique.

FLUGELHORN (*plate 3*)

The flugelhorn is a wider-bored conical instrument in B♭, with technically the same compass as the cornet, but is generally used in brass bands to produce a rather warmer tone in the middle and lower registers than can be achieved on the cornet or trumpet. There is normally only one flugel in a full band.

HORN (*plate 4*)

The orchestral horn is referred to as the 'French' horn, despite the fact that the modern wide-bored, F/B♭, rotary-valved instrument is probably more properly called a 'German' horn. Players of this instrument insist on its being called a 'horn' and nothing else, although the term 'double horn' (for the F/B♭ instrument) is now quite common. At the same time the term 'horn' means a quite different instrument to the brass band player, for the same word is used to identify the tenor saxhorn in E♭. In this book 'horn' means the orchestral instrument, and 'tenor horn' the band instrument.

Modern horns mostly come in two forms: the single F horn, or the double F/B♭ horn (which is really two horns in one, with a switch for changing from one to the other). The horn is a narrow tubed, conical-bore instrument with a very wide flare at the bell. Technically its compass is:

In practice, however, the most comfortable range is:

TENOR HORN (*plate 5*)

The tenor saxhorn in E♭, of which there are usually three in a brass band, has a much wider bore than the orchestral horn,

and uses the cup-shaped mouthpiece of the other band
instruments, instead of the funnel-shaped one so characteristic
of the orchestral horn. Compass:

It will be noticed, therefore, that the orchestral horn can cover
the range of the tenor horn. The possibility of its use in the
brass band sector is discussed in chapter 6.

BARITONE HORN (*plate 6*)

The baritone saxhorn in B♭, of which there are usually two in
a brass band, is, of course, another member of the saxhorn
family (of which further members are sometimes encountered
on the continent, but not normally in Great Britain). Like the
tenor horn, the baritone is a wide-bore instrument with three
valves, and it has a similar range both in terms of pitch and
dynamics. Like the tenor horn also, it does not normally find a
place outside the brass band. Compass (which doubles that of
the tenor trombone):

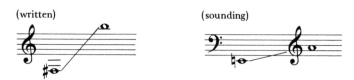

EUPHONIUM (*plate 7*)

The euphonium, or tenor tuba as it is usually called in the
orchestra, is now usually built with a fourth valve, so that it

can command a fairly extensive compass:

(Orchestral parts are normally written in C in the bass and tenor clefs, but for the brass band the euphonium is a treble-clef instrument, transposing down a major ninth, like the baritone.) The bore of the euphonium is wider than that of the baritone, and thus its tone is much fuller.

TROMBONE (*plate 8*)

The instrument most likely to be encountered in schools today is the tenor trombone, with a compass of

However, many players possess the B♭/F instrument which gives them an additional range of bottom E natural to B♭:

These instruments are manufactured both as tenor and bass instruments: the wider-bored bass instruments do not, however, have a lower compass, for both instruments are built in B♭. (The old bass trombone in G, though occasionally still found in some brass bands, is in effect obsolete.) The bass B♭/F is designed simply to give the lower part of the trombone's compass more weight.

Orchestral players read their parts in C in the bass and tenor clefs, while band players read 'tenor' parts in the treble clef (i.e. with a major ninth transposition), and the 'bass' parts in the bass clef. The trombone, like the trumpet, has a cylindrical bore for most of its length, only broadening out towards the widely flared bell.

TUBA (*plate 9*)

Apart from the euphonium or tenor tuba, the three tubas which are in common use are:

F tuba   E♭ tuba   BB♭ tuba

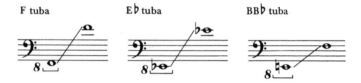

Only four-valved tubas can fill the gap between the lowest note of the second harmonic and the fundamental, so three-valved instruments have a gap in their compass between the fundamental and the augmented fourth of the scale. Four-valved BB♭ tubas are rare. The F instrument is the traditional orchestral tuba, but many orchestral players now use whichever is the most appropriate instrument for the part. Band players read their parts in the treble clef, transposing an octave and a major sixth for the E♭, and two octaves and a major second for the BB♭. Orchestral players read all parts in the bass clef.

3 Clefs and Transpositions

Although the normal transpositions for brass parts have been briefly indicated in the previous chapter, the whole problem causes so much bewilderment to many people that it is probably worth while to look at the situation in a little more detail. The following diagram may help to indicate the extent of the problem:

In order to sound the note

parts must be written as follows:

E♭ cornet

B♭ trumpet/cornet/flugelhorn

F Horn

E♭ Tenor Horn

Baritone Horn/Euphonium 𝄞/Tenor Trombone 𝄞

Trombone 𝄢 / Euphonium 𝄢 / Tuba 𝄢

E♭ Tuba(Bass) 𝄞

BB♭ Tuba (Bass) 𝄞

*Of course the BB♭ bass does not actually play as high as this!

It can be seen that we have inherited a very complicated notational problem. Basically these systems of notation have grown up for the convenience of the player, so that the fingering on valved instruments is always the same. There is a certain strength in this argument when it is applied to the instruments whose compass is more or less within the confines of the treble clef. Thus it is obviously desirable that the trumpet player can switch from B♭ to C to D instrument and employ the same fingering. Historically, the same would have applied to the orchestral horn, but the twentieth-century standardization of the F horn has undermined the reason for retaining transposing notation for this instrument. However, the value of bass instruments reading from the treble clef is very doubtful. The traditional brass band view has been that players must be able to shift from instrument to instrument as the need arises, and thus players should be able to move freely from the treble cornet parts to the alto horn parts, to the tenor euphonium parts and so on to the bass parts. Such an idea, though superficially attractive, overlooks the basic problems that occur for a player in adjusting to mouthpieces of different sizes and different shapes. Although some players may be able to adapt quickly to a larger mouthpiece, very few can cope with the problems of a smaller one without a great deal of experience. In reality there is not a great deal of movement from one instrument to another, at least not in bands that are interested in tone quality.

It would not be unreasonable, therefore, to encourage all tenor horn, baritone, euphonium, trombone, and tuba players to read from non-transposing parts in the tenor and bass clefs. The case of the trombone is quite extraordinary in the present situation. The argument of transferability makes no sense whatsoever as applied to the tenor trombone in a band. Cornet, horn, or bass players can hardly be expected to pick up the slide technique overnight, so the ability to read the part in the treble clef is irrelevant in any case. Much more important is the need to be able to pass from tenor to bass trombone parts as the need arises, and yet in the band the tenor parts are transposing and the bass parts are not.

The normal practice today is for trombone players to learn the orchestral way. That is, they start by learning the bass clef and join the band as bass trombonists. Then when they have mastered the tenor clef, which is always taught to trombone players from about Grade three level, they are shown how to read treble clef parts as if they were in the tenor clef. Thus:

for the B♭
transposing
instrument.

It will be seen that because the notes on the tenor clef non-transposing part lie in the same position on the stave as the treble clef transposing part, the player experienced in the tenor clef can easily read from the treble clef. All he has to do is substitute mentally a tenor clef for the treble clef and make the necessary adjustments to the key signature, which is simply achieved by adding two flats to (or removing two sharps from) the treble clef part. E.g.

would be read as

This technique can easily be applied also to the baritone and the euphonium, and the use of the bass and tenor clefs is as valid for them as it is for the trombone. It is sometimes argued that young players should not be confused by the appearance of two clefs: such a view overlooks the fact that young pianists employ two clefs all the time. If baritone and euphonium players are to be able to take a full part in brass music outside the band as well as inside it, they will have to become fluent readers of the bass clef in any case. Players of these instruments who can only read from the treble clef are prisoners of the system.

The case for tuba players reading from the bass clef could not be stronger. Quite apart from the fact that a transposition as wide as two octaves and a second gives the player a very unreal sense of the actual pitch of his part, it is again essential that tuba players should be equally at home in the band and the orchestra, and indeed be able to play bass trombone parts where appropriate. It should be noted, however, that E♭ tuba parts in the treble clef can easily be read as non-transposing bass clef parts simply by imagining a bass clef and adding three flats to (or removing three sharps from) the key signature.

Reforms in notation often appear more difficult to achieve than breaking into the Bank of England: however, it must be remembered that constant pressure eventually overcame the brass bands' resistance to the change to a lower standard pitch, and that continuous pressure from the consumer might have the appropriate effect on publishers today. It is educationally highly undesirable that young players should be prevented from moving from one type of music to another simply because of totally unnecessary complications in notational systems.

It is appropriate to point out here that, as the school music teacher rummages through old music stock in his cupboards, he is likely to come across a number of other notational eccentricities: horn parts in C, D, E♭, and B♭; trumpet parts in A or F (in addition to those in B♭, C, D, and E♭); and (rarely) trombone parts in the alto clef. Properly trained brass players are used to transposing as an everyday activity, but there is often no alternative in schools to the laborious process of writing out transposed parts. Well organized secondary school teachers give this task to 'O' level candidates in order to show them that transposition has some purpose: it is essential, however, that such work is carried out with accuracy and clarity, for a badly written-out transposition is worse than no transposition at all.

The following examples of brass arrangements with conventional transpositions are included for the benefit of those readers new to the problems:

J.S.Bach: Chorale
Jesu, meine Freude

Arranged for two trumpets, horn, and trombone
If the music is to be played at the same pitch, then the trumpets end up in an 'awkward' key, with E sharps:

1st trumpet in B♭

2nd trumpet in B♭

Horn in F

Trombone

*Horn parts often appear without key signatures

It would be much better in this example to put the music down a tone, thus:

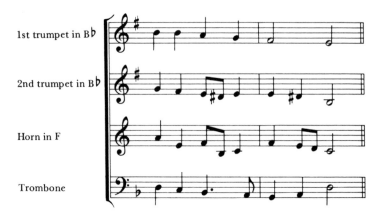

Arranged for flugelhorn, tenor horn, euphonium, and bass (again transposed down a tone).

Arranged for trumpet in C, horn in F, trombone, and tuba (bass clef, non-transposing) *in the original key of E minor:*

*Many horn parts still appear without key signatures, despite much advice to the contrary.

4 Instruments in Small Groups

Brass solo with piano

The published repertoire of pieces for a brass instrument with piano accompaniment is very extensive indeed, which is surprising, for it is in this context that brass instruments are least well known. We are all familiar with the role of the brass section in the symphony orchestra, the handful of concertos for brass instruments, and the band repertoire; we are also becoming increasingly familiar with the ensemble repertoire; but examples of concert performances of music for a solo instrument with piano are very rare indeed.

Why, then, is there such a large repertoire? The answer appears to involve the place of examinations and auditions in the activities of young players. For every graded examination system, for every conservatoire prize competition, for every entrance examination or festival, lists of solos appear, and 'suitable' works for such occasions accumulate year after year. Of course, many such pieces are simply piano reductions of orchestral material, and thus few people would prefer, for example, to hear the Mozart horn concertos played on horn and piano, when they can regularly be heard played in their proper form with orchestra.

Of the many pieces written as *original* works for brass solo and piano, alarmingly few are by major composers, and many of those which come into this category are in any case too difficult for the average school player. For the horn, for example, the list of original works with piano by major composers might include Beethoven's *Sonata in F*, Op. 17, Dukas's *Villanelle*, Fricker's *Sonata*, Op. 24, Hamilton's *Sonata notturna*, Hindemith's *Sonata* (1939), Lutyens's *Duo*, Poulenc's *Elegie*, Rossini's *Rondo fantastique*, Saint-Saëns's

Romance, Op. 67, and Schumann's *Adagio and Allegro*, Op. 70. This is clearly not a very impressive list, but it is superior, if anything, to similar lists for the trumpet or the trombone.

Reductions for solo and piano of works for solo brass and orchestra undoubtedly provide some excellent material for players in schools, although only an exceptional player can manage all the movements of some works. Generations of good young players have been brought up on the concertos of Mozart, Haydn, Hummel, Rimsky-Korsakov, and Strauss, but they can hardly be said to fulfil the same needs that the sonata repertoire does in the case of the violin or the cello. In order to build up the solo repertoire many composers have turned their attention to the musical problems involved, but few of them are sufficiently well known to command immediate attention. Teachers and pupils must therefore be prepared to engage in a constant process of selection and rejection in order to find material that is worth playing. Music by German, French, and American composers is particularly plentiful in this field, ranging from short semi-descriptive pieces to full-scale sonatas.

Arrangements, for solo brass and piano, of many hundreds of pieces not initially conceived for either instrument have nevertheless provided many players with a great deal of pleasure. It is often fascinating to hear how the skill of the arranger can make a Handel operatic aria, a Bach cantata, an Elizabethan virginal piece, a theme from a Beethoven symphony, a Schubert song, a Wagner chorus, a Tchaikovsky ballet movement, or an Elgar march into a presentable item for the young performer's repertoire. In selecting material from this sector, the teacher should keep the following questions in mind: does the arrangement provide the player with material appropriate for the next stage of his development, and is it likely to extend his knowledge of musical literature?

The qualities of an arrangement should also be investigated from the pianist's point of view, for it is often on this side that problems occur. Some reductions of orchestral material are very un-pianistic, and make demands upon the pianist quite out of proportion to his role as 'accompanist'. Others have failed to ensure the sort of balance that will assist the inexperienced soloist. The circumstances surrounding the preparation of accompanied solos also needs very careful scrutiny. Generally speaking, it is safe to say that the sooner the two players meet and practise together, the better will be their chances of developing some sort of working relationship. Not all brass teachers are also competent pianists, and it is therefore a matter for the permanent music staff of the school to arrange for the availability of accompanists. Sometimes it will be members of staff who themselves take on the responsibility for this sort of work, but it is of course highly desirable that other young players should be given the opportunity to take a full part in this vitally important musical activity.

No doubt there are many very simple arrangements in which no great harm is done if the pianist joins the soloist at the last stage of his preparation, but in many arrangements, and certainly in the major original works, the piano has its own important contribution to make to the partnership, and all the questions of phrasing, tempo, and dynamics need to be thought out for the piece as a whole, not just for one of the two performers. It is a particularly valuable experience for the pianist to develop an instinct for ensemble music, for much too often he leads a musically self-centred life, never having to listen to others as he plays.

In the rush of school life the problems of arranging for players to meet together regularly, possibly under supervision, seem to provide just one more headache in an already overcrowded week. Nevertheless, teachers who believe such activities to be important will find a way of ensuring that they take place. Regular provision of rehearsal facilities is an essential characteristic of a serious approach to musical education, and it applies as much to young players in junior schools as it does to those in secondary schools.

Undoubtedly the trumpet and horn have the best solo and piano repertoire, and music for these instruments can make interesting contributions to school concerts. The trombone has received a great deal of attention in recent years, and where the music has been thought out in real trombone/piano textures, some splendid material is available; but when the trombone part is merely a trumpet part played an octave lower, one is forced to wonder if the arranger has any feeling whatsoever for sonorities and textures. As for the tuba and piano, one cannot do better than quote Mary Rasmussen's famous observation: 'No one ever claimed that the tuba had any solo repertory; and for this reason, if for no other, one should think twice before consigning anyone to the tuba player's fate. Besides, the combination of tuba and piano is sheer madness. Tuba players play with piano like lemmings march to the sea, out of blind, suicidal tradition. Nobody wants to be left out.'[1]

Brass duets
Music for two instruments of the same type is not only available in the form of specially composed or arranged music for those instruments, but also from scores originally produced for singers, or recorders, or clarinets, or whatever. Whether or not such music ever rises above the level of exercises is open to discussion. Playing such duet material is obviously a valuable teaching resource, but concert material usually depends upon other musical characteristics.

Plenty of duets are now also available for two different instruments, some of which are worth hearing more than once. It is not, however, until three instruments get together that any real signs of music occur.

[1] Rasmussen, M. *A teacher's guide to the literature of brass instruments*, 2nd ed. (Durham, New Hampshire, 1968), p. 59.

Brass Trios

As with duets, there are plenty of possibilities for trios of like instruments to play either music especially arranged, or music intended for other instruments or voices. It is, however, when one thinks of trios of mixed instruments that the repertoire begins to look interesting. The trio combinations that seem to work best are those consisting of two trumpets and trombone, and of trumpet, horn, and trombone, and it is for this latter group that Poulenc wrote his well known *Sonata* (1922).

Brass Quartets

Whereas the term 'string quartet' has a standard meaning, 'brass quartet' may suggest two trumpets/horn/trombone or two trumpets/two trombones or, in the brass band world, two cornets/tenor horn/euphonium (or trombone). In all its forms, however, the brass quartet is rich in repertoire both in original works and in arrangements. Among modern British composers, works by John Addison, John Gardner, Gordon Jacob, John McCabe, and Richard Stoker are well worth exploring. For most school quartets, however, the staple diet is drawn from the Venetian canzona repertoire, which boasts many superb works by the Gabrielis and their contemporaries, including the Germans Scheidt and Schein. There are also many excellent arrangements of later baroque works which include pieces by Bach, Handel, and Purcell.

Quartets of like instruments also provide plenty of interesting music, but the trombone quartet is perhaps the most rewarding. Four trombones in many ways produce one of the most satisfying sounds in brass music: sonorous, flexible, subtle in intonation, and capable of great breadth of expression. Many modern writers have been quick to exploit its virtues, and arrangers have taken advantage of the delights of late renaissance and baroque counterpoint to produce scores of undeniable charm.

The establishment of regularly rehearsing quartets within

the school is a sure sign of a healthy brass section. Such a quartet needs not less than an hour's supervised rehearsal each week, and an ever-expanding supply of worthwhile music to perform.

Brass Quintets

It is arguable that the quintet has the best repertoire of all the brass groups. Among modern works there are fine examples from Malcolm Arnold, Eugene Bozza, Peter Dickinson, Iain Hamilton, Paul Hindemith, Joseph Horovitz, John McCabe, and Bernard Stevens. From the 'transcribed' list there are great riches to be found in the works of Adson, Bach, Coleman, Melchior Franck, Holborne, Pezel, Scheidt, Schein, and Speer. It is not an overstatement to say that even a very good school quintet would be hard pressed to get through a small part of the available repertoire.

If a 'standard' quintet can be said to exist, then it is made up of two trumpets, horn, trombone, and tuba. However, the quintet of two trumpets and three trombones is almost as common, and obviously various other combinations have appealed to composers and arrangers from time to time. It is, perhaps, worth stressing at this point that the tuba part in a quintet is an independent, freely moving part quite different in nature from the normal orchestral or band parts that tuba players are called upon to play. A four-valved euphonium (tenor tuba) is often a useful member of the brass quintet, although the larger F or E♭ instruments more often find a place.

A good quintet should have not only a fine sonorous tone, but also a buoyant sense of rhythm. Although the quintet has the physical power to produce a good deal of volume, most of its work involves the more subtle, softer dynamics. Clear phrasing and light textures help to create the appropriate sense of ensemble that every quintet must endeavour to develop. A quintet that contains a horn must necessarily model its sense of dynamics on the horn and not on the more incisive tone of the cylindrically constructed trumpets and trombones. Many quintets make the mistake of forcing the horn to 'play up' to such a level that good tone quality is quite impossible for all but the very experienced player. It is always more appropriate in school contexts for the trumpets and trombones to shade down their dynamics rather than to ask the horn player to play in an uncharacteristic manner.

As has already been pointed out in the context of quartets, the quintet must meet regularly if it is to develop that sense of interdependence among its players that is so essential to good ensemble music. No doubt it is often the case that the quintet is simply the regular quartet plus one more player; but good quintet playing cannot be developed on a sort of 'guest artist' basis, for the arrival of the fifth player completely changes the balance within the group. Very careful coaching is absolutely essential: the role of the teacher here is to lend a pair of experienced ears to the operation. Of course, the players will themselves gradually develop a sense of balance within the group, but someone who can stand back and listen to the complete sound of the quintet, and make sensible suggestions on how matters of balance and phrasing can be improved, is a great asset to any ensemble.

Rehearsal accommodation is always a problem with the larger ensembles, and the quintet needs a room which is large enough not to box up the sound, but not so large that the players feel they have to behave like a full band. Properly equipped music departments in the larger schools will, of course, have rooms of different sizes to accommodate such requirements, but in the majority of schools many such rehearsals will no doubt continue to take place in ordinary classrooms with the desks moved aside.

Sextets and larger groups

Brass ensemble music is available in considerable profusion right up to the traditional limits of chamber-music proportions – the nonet. Chamber-music conditions (that is, one instrument to each part) also apply to music for much larger groups: the triple quintets of Gabrieli, for example. (There is even the famous 22-part *Sonata* of Gabrieli which, technically, fulfils chamber-music specifications!) Music for double quartets is particularly common, and provides an admirable opportunity for two school quartets to play together on special occasions. The nearer the numbers approach the proportions of ᵗhe band, however, the less is the opportunity offered to the players to develop a real chamber-music approach to their ensemble playing.

5 Developing an Ensemble Repertoire

In the first chapter, one of the general arguments presented in support of the development of brass teaching in schools was that there is available to the player a sufficient body of music of considerable merit. If the teacher requires acceptable answers to both the questions 'can it be played?' and 'is it worth playing?', then he must satisfy himself that within the available brass repertoire there is music that is as satisfying to the brass player as are, for example, the string quartets of Mozart to the string player, or the madrigals of Marenzio to the singer, or the waltzes of Chopin to the pianist.

Attempts to justify the musical worth of brass music usually begin with arguments in support of the valuable contribution of the Venetians. Strictly speaking, the Venetian School dates from Adrian Willaert (c. 1490–1562), who worked in St. Mark's from about 1527. It included a great number of Flemish as well as Italian composers. The most important figures were Cipriano de Rore (1516–65), Andrea Gabrieli (c. 1520–86), Giovanni Gabrieli (1557–1612), Giovanni Croce (c. 1557–1609), and Claudio Merulo (1533–1604). The Venetian influence was also very strong in Germany and Austria, where Jacobus Gallus or Handl (1550–91), Hieronymus Praetorius (1560–1629), Michael Praetorius (1571–1621), and Hans Leo Hassler (1564–1612) were pre-eminent. The ensemble works written towards the end of this period are of most interest to the brass player.

The ensemble repertoire, however, is by no means limited to music of the past. The growth in composition for brass ensembles in the twentieth century is very marked. Not only have many first-rank composers written for various combinations of brass instruments, but first-rate works for brass have also been written by composers not widely known outside the brass repertoire (see Chapter 4). It is not unreasonable to suggest that the brass player has available to him as fine a collection of ensemble music as the woodwind player.

The real problem, in terms of programme-building, faced by the brass ensemble is the considerable gap that lies between the standard Venetian repertoire and the modern repertoire; so when it comes to persuading other musicians of the value of brass ensemble music, one is put on the defensive in terms of eighteenth- and nineteenth-century pieces. Some suspicion is comprehensible, in the context of popular musical history; people have been brought up to associate the great achievements of Western European music with a fairly limited period — that of the conventional Bach—Beethoven—Brahms triumvirate. Such a view is particularly prevalent among pianists, who tend to be predominant in schools. Nevertheless, just as the pianist-teachers are able, often with very great success, to extend their interests and enthusiasms to vocal and orchestral works, so also are they able to encompass the repertoire of both the pre-Bach and post-Brahms periods. As far as brass ensemble music is concerned, it is precisely in these periods that the major repertoire lies.

For the school, however, the absence of eighteenth- and nineteenth-century repertoire can be turned to advantage. In the first place, the activities of the brass ensemble dovetail very effectively with other ensembles likely to be found in schools, for whom the 1700—1900 era will produce the basic repertoire. In the second, the absence of material should encourage the arranger to get to work in order to provide some appropriate material from this period. It must be hoped, however, that such enthusiasm will be tempered by discretion.

When one asserts that the brass music of the twentieth century includes some fine works, one must inevitably go on to say that much of it is also very demanding of the players, just as the great works in the piano repertoire are very demanding of pianists. Some of the Venetian music is also very difficult, but, equally, a great deal of it is quite approachable by young players. The problem that one is more likely to encounter in connection with this period is the demand for authenticity of performance. This should not be allowed to stop young people playing great works of art with whatever means they have at their command. While it is true that the Venetian cornetts and sackbuts sound very different from modern, more powerful brass instruments, it is also true that the modern instruments can present Venetian music in a very satisfying manner. Given the choice between playing the Venetians on modern instruments or not at all, who would hesitate in his choice? Who would prevent young people playing Bach on the piano, an instrument as different from its eighteenth-century predecessors as the modern brass instruments are from their seventeenth-century ancestors?

It is sometimes argued that the spirit of the music is best preserved in performances which have *mixed* groups of instruments, i.e. strings, woodwind, and possibly a keyboard instrument. One of the more obvious possibilities lies in the use of clarinets in some of the parts. Two points may be noted in this connection: first, the use of clarinets does not make the music sound any more 'authentic', for clarinets arrived two hundred years too late for this purpose; second, clarinets are no real match for brass instruments in power, especially in their lower registers, where they are often asked to 'fill in' trombone or low trumpet parts. As far as strings are concerned, so many strings per part are needed to balance the brass that the whole spirit of chamber music is lost.

For those players who do set aside prejudice and ignorance, and really get down to familiarizing themselves with the instrumental works of the Venetians, there are considerable rewards in store. There are works for many possible combinations of instruments, and with imagination and a willingness to experiment, most school brass groups will find pieces among the collection that will provide them with many hours of pleasure. There are not only many works for regular playing by small groups, but some spectacular pieces for larger combinations that can be played at festivals or on other occasions when there are plenty of players available.

Players who tackle this type of music must realize, however, that they have to approach the music in a manner which is rather different from the one that most players will have been accustomed to in orchestras and bands. Playing Venetian brass music is essentially like playing chamber music, and everyone involved must develop a spirit of inter-dependence in rehearsal and performance. Some of the problems were well described by Denis Arnold when he wrote that the players must be 'willing to adopt a new attitude towards the problems presented by the music. Just as it would be absolutely disastrous to make five opera singers into a madrigal group without a great deal of adaptation and education, so it is equally unsatisfactory to expect brass and woodwind players used to performing harmonic music in a mainly nineteenth- and twentieth-century tradition to natur-ally make sixteenth-century music interesting and authentic-sounding. They will have to learn a new method of phrasing, to acquire a new understanding of rhythm. Above all, they will have to learn to listen to other parts more carefully, and to comprehend the structure of the piece.'[1]

It is likely that many players will wish to establish their repertoire by getting to know the major works of the Venetians, and in particular the works of Giovanni Gabrieli. Readers should therefore turn to the Appendix – 'The Canzonas of Giovanni Gabrieli' – for more detailed advice.

---

[1] Arnold, D. 'Con ogni sorte di stromenti: some practical suggestions'; *Brass Quarterly*, II (1958), p. 108.

6 The Brass Band

When one moves from the larger brass ensembles to the brass band one enters a ritualistic, carefully preserved territory that many musicians find completely incomprehensible. For a start, there are instruments not normally encountered elsewhere: the cornet, the flugelhorn, the tenor horn, and the baritone. Then there are the strange transpositions already referred to in Chapter 3; the odd nomenclature, with some of the first cornets known as *solos*, and the rest known as *repiano* (instead of ripieno) cornets; the inconsistency in the use of clefs, with the bass trombone alone playing in the bass clef; the determination of certain organizations to prevent trumpets and (French) horns from participating in competitions; the preponderance of lower-pitched instruments; the fondness for a *vibrato* style of playing; the fascination of the majority of conductors with pieces designed solely for the display of technique; and, last but by no means least, the widespread enthusiasm for arrangements of music that had few claims to preservation in its original form, let alone in its adapted form.

The brass band conspicuously has its own traditions. It grew up quite outside the professional world of music in the nineteenth century, and although many contacts have been established with other branches of music-making in the twentieth century, it is essentially its independence which continues to characterize its way of life. Until well after the end of the Second World War brass bands continued to employ a concert pitch higher than the internationally agreed concert pitch, to which all orchestral instruments were tuned. This has inevitably meant that, for the greater part of this century, no easy transition from band to orchestra has been possible.

Perhaps the most important element of its tradition is a

social one. Brass bands grew up as essentially working-class institutions, and are even today particularly associated with the major industrial regions of the British Isles. There was no reason why bands should not act independently of orchestras for the simple reason that there were no points of contact between them. The players in the brass bands only played in their spare time, as often as not as a relief from the rigours of nineteenth-century industrial life. It was usually the factory or works band in any case, with the money for the instruments and the uniforms originating from the owners, and taking the form of a type of advertising or rudimentary personnel management scheme.

During recent times, however, the position has changed in some important respects. In the first place, many fine players from the bands have developed their interests more widely, and are at home both in the (theoretically) amateur world of the brass band and the professional worlds of dance bands and orchestras. Secondly, there has been a movement away from the social divisions associated with bands and orchestras, and good players have been happy to play wherever there has been an opportunity to take part in music-making at a serious level.

The latter point is particularly significant in the school context. No teacher would now regard the band as a socially unacceptable element in the school's activities. On the contrary, the brass band has now established a firm place in musical education, and is valued for the many assets which it possesses. As has already been mentioned, the competition band is a great social and educational force, bringing people together who might otherwise have little social contact, and encouraging them to achieve group standards that could hardly have been thought of for individual players. Because of the style of scoring, the band has a built-in apprenticeship scheme for developing the skills of its players, with the new players happily supported by the more experienced. The eleven-year-old can play in the same band as the eighteen-year-old without spoiling the latter's enjoyment, and he can also recognize his own progress as he develops his own self-confidence and takes a gradually more responsible role in the band.

Unlike any other form of music-making, the activities of the brass band are controlled to a very great extent by the rules of brass band contests. The length and type of pieces played are often decided in this way, and the make-up of the band is similarly determined by external factors. About twenty-four players are specified:

1	soprano E♭ cornet	2	B♭ baritone horns
4/5	solo B♭ cornets	3	trombones
1	repiano B♭ cornet	1 or 2	euphoniums
1	flugelhorn	1 or 2	E♭ basses
2	2nd B♭ cornets	1 or 2	BB♭ basses
2	3rd B♭ cornets	(Percussion)	
2/3	E♭ horns		

Of course there can be variations, and some bands prefer to give more weight to some sections and less to others. In practice, many bands regularly rehearse with more players so that they can have plenty of 'reserves' for competitions. It is inevitable that phrases borrowed from the world of sport enter into the description of brass bands, for the 'sports' element in band playing is never far from the surface. This competitive atmosphere can be both to the advantage and to the disadvantage of the players. In so far as the contest tends to make players work hard at their playing, and develops a strong sense of loyalty, obvious good accrues; but when the contest is allowed to determine both what shall be played and when it shall be played, regardless of musical value or educational purpose, then clearly the best musical interests of young players are being overlooked.

The sound of the brass band is essentially a blended one: with the sole exception of the cylindrical-bore trombones, the band is made up of conical-bore instruments. This makes it

1. Bb trumpet

2. Bb cornet

3. B♭ flugelhorn

4. Double horn

5. E♭ tenor horn

6. Baritone horn

7. 4-valve euphonium

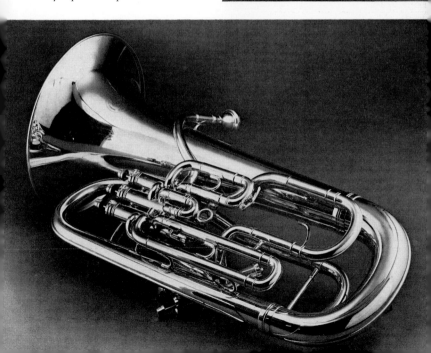

8. B♮/F trombone

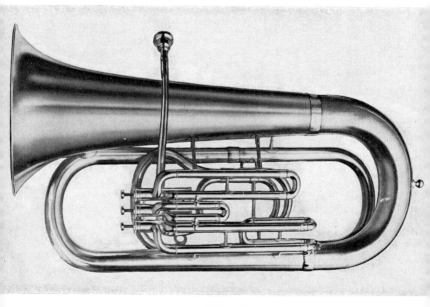

9. BB♮ tuba

possible for the band to produce a rich, warm, round tone in which no one group of instruments stands out. Even the trombones are encouraged to employ a style of playing in which any incisiveness is studiously avoided. Furthermore, there is a distribution of instruments which gives far more emphasis to the lower registers than is usual, for example, in the standard orchestra. With only one soprano cornet the band is not equipped to provide for the sort of work that can be accomplished by violins, flutes, or even clarinets. The massive power of the bass instruments often leads to over-emphasis of the lower registers, with a tendency towards thick-textured writing for horns, baritones, trombones, and tubas.

It is perhaps unnecessary to point out that the best scoring for brass band takes into account the nature of the band itself, and does not attempt to re-allocate orchestral parts to unsuitable instruments. It is pointless to think in terms of the cornets behaving like first and second violins, or the baritones taking on the cello part, or whatever. Scoring for brass bands is based on entirely different principles from orchestral scoring. It follows, therefore, that music originally conceived for orchestra does not always transfer to the band with any degree of comfort. In the context of the school band it is particularly important that the players are provided with music that is well fitted to their abilities: even though the best cornet players from the prize-winning bands can cope with pseudo-string or pseudo-woodwind parts, there is no real excuse for forcing such parts on young players.

Most school brass players enjoy their role in the band, for it provides them with much more continuous participation than they often find in the orchestra. However hard a conductor may try to sustain the interest of his young brass players in orchestral music, it is inevitable that the strings will demand most of his attention, and that the trumpets and trombones will have a great many empty bars to count. One cannot but sympathize with the player who, after counting his forty-nine bars rest, raises his instrument to his lips only to be stopped at the very point of entry so that the passage can be rehearsed again.

From the point of view of the young player's development, therefore, it is highly desirable that he should be able to play in both the orchestra and the band. Unfortunately, many obstacles seem to be placed in his path. Although trumpets are freely employed in bands, the regulations for some competitions at the national level demand cornets and not trumpets, and so many players are forced into a position where they play either in the band or the orchestra, but not both. Again, in spite of many attempts to make changes, the French horn is not welcomed in most bands; there are no F-transposed parts in most sets of band parts for a start, and many bandmasters view the instrument with some suspicion. Although trombone players experienced in reading the tenor clef can easily adapt the band parts written in the treble clef, this does represent yet another hurdle to be overcome. Transfer between orchestra and band for the tuba player means more reading complications.

Perhaps the biggest problem is the central matter of tone quality. Although it is not true of the best bands today, there has been for a considerable time a strong inclination towards a vibrato style of playing in bands which orchestral brass teachers cannot tolerate. Many such teachers have often gone so far as to refuse to allow their pupils to play in brass bands in which this, now mostly obsolete, style of playing still obtains. It is only too easy for the young player to pick up a manner of playing which it may take years of careful teaching to eradicate at a later stage.

Today, of course, some of the best players have band as well as orchestral experience, and the demands made upon these players in contest bands are such that their advanced technical achievements fit them for all types of music. In the school situation, however, it is vital that players can concentrate on the development of their musicianship without experiencing the strains of having to produce different types of playing for different situations.

Many people would like to see the orchestral brass —
trumpets, horns, trombones, and tubas — encouraged to
participate in the world of the band without having to modify
their style of playing (i.e. tone quality), and without having to
adjust to different forms of notation. It is true that such a
change would imply a fundamental alteration in brass band
procedures, but the brass band's resistance to new ideas is one
of its least endearing characteristics. If, in other words, the
brass band were to become merely an extension of the larger
brass ensembles, then there would be fewer problems
associated with the development of brass music in schools.

While the trumpet, horn, trombone, or tuba player may
theoretically have access to both the orchestra and the band,
the position of players brought up on the tenor horn, the
baritone, or the euphonium is less clear. These instruments
have no recognized place in orchestral music (with the possible
exception of the tenor tuba parts in some big orchestral
scores). The technique of the tenor and baritone saxhorns is
quite different from the orchestral horn, and so it is not
possible for players to exchange instruments. They can
participate in brass ensemble music, always provided that they
can overcome transposition problems, but in many respects
players of these instruments, though often fine players in their
own right, can find no outlet for their abilities except the
band.

It may well be that some players will be quite satisfied with
their role in bands, and have no desire to play in other forms
of music, but in view of the limitations in repertoire which
exist for the band, such an attitude cannot determine the
educational objectives of music in schools. There are two
obvious solutions to the problem: either tenor and baritone
horn players should also play a second (orchestral) instrument,
or the role of these instruments should be replaced altogether
in the brass band. There can be little doubt that the orchestral
horn, especially the modern double horn, is well equipped to
cope with most of the material given to the saxhorns, and
what is left over might well be given to the tenor tuba. One has

fewer qualms about starting a young player on the euphonium, for it forms a reasonable introduction to the tuba family, particularly if it is taught as a bass clef instrument.

Such changes in the instrumentation of bands are long overdue, and just as the band organizations were slow to adopt modern concert pitch, they have also been slow to adopt a more flexible approach to matters of scoring.[1] It is the composer who should have the final word in the instrumentation of his music; and no doubt if the band organizations were more adaptable in this respect, many more composers would feel that they could write in a way which provided them with the normal freedoms of the composer. Although there have been some outstanding contributions to the repertoire from composers like Elgar, Holst, Bliss, Ireland, Vaughan Williams, and Arnold, there has been a marked lack of interest from others such as Walton, Tippett, Rawsthorne, Berkeley, and Britten. Outside Great Britain the major composers have had hardly any contact with the brass band, and so the repertoire lacks its Stravinsky, Bartók, Schoenberg, Berg, Hindemith, and Janaček, in spite of the fact that all these composers have written with conspicuous brilliance for brass in other contexts. Because band players have no way of approaching at first hand the music of the major composers of the first half of the twentieth century, let alone the avant-garde of the second half, a deep-rooted suspicion of most modern music is characteristic of many band circles. It may of course, be argued that the function of the brass band is, like a museum, to preserve various historical traditions; but if one believes that musical education is concerned with other matters, and in particular with the development of the musical imagination, then one must hope that the brass band world will do everything possible to come to terms with the present.

[1] The Guildhall School Brass Ensemble, in London, is an example of the type of re-orchestration that is possible, with trumpets replacing cornets (except for the E♭ Soprano and the Flugel), and French horns replacing saxhorns.

The brass band is an institution well within the grasp of all secondary schools, and not very far from the reach of upper juniors and middle schools. It can provide worthwhile ensemble experience for players in the early stages of their musical development as well as for experienced players. It has the resources to fill the largest school halls with sound, and even to adapt to outdoor conditions. It is useful in assemblies and ceremonial occasions. Before the days of the amplifier and powerful speakers it was the main source of outdoor music, and it still has a role to play in this respect. Although formerly a male preserve, it now rejoices in the contribution of players from both sexes. It has a social function of indisputable significance, and an educational role of considerable force. The time has come for it to assert its serious musical values.

As far as the existing repertoire is concerned, the catalogues of several publishers who have a heavy commitment in this field provide the school band with a considerable variety of arrangements and a few original works of merit. Some of this music is adapted from military band scores, and marches and quick-moving overtures make particularly good material for school use. Pieces that make use of national dance rhythms, especially Caribbean and South American ones, also prove very successful, as do arrangements of interesting folk-song material. Less successful in the school context are those scores which string together a number of tunes from West End musicals, or other so-called 'light music'. Such music may still hold attractions for the devotees of the seaside bandstand, but it is as foreign to most children as the Victorian ballads that were so cherished by their great-grandparents. At one time the brass band repertoire included a large number of arrangements of the 'classics'; since it is now very easy for anyone to listen to these works in their original form, the need for brass band versions no longer seems very great. The brass band in the role of popularizer now seems particularly redundant.

One must be particularly wary of music with a 'funny' title — 'Troublesome tubas' or 'Flirtatious flugelhorns' or the like. In many such pieces the rest of the band play um-pa-pa to accompany the acrobatics of an often unlikely soloist. It is very difficult to understand why anyone should wish to perform music of such monumental triviality, let alone in an educational setting. The school band can build up a repertoire of worthwhile pieces that will give satisfaction to players and listeners alike without having to waste everyone's time and energy on such rubbish.

Building up a good concert repertoire is a long-term operation, and involves a great deal of careful scrutiny of scores. Many bandmasters have been known to perform pieces for no better reason than that the music cupboard contains sets of parts, however old or however unsuitable to present requirements they may be. The head of a music department in a large school has a particular responsibility in this context. He himself may not rehearse the band, and may even employ the services of a bandmaster who is not on the full-time staff of the school. It is essential, however, that he plays a full part in the development of the band as an element of the total pattern of musical education in the school, and that he takes some personal interest in the selection of repertoire. Many very fine bandmasters are unfamiliar with trends in modern musical education, or with the general twentieth-century repertoire outside their own field, and it is quite understandable why this should be the case. There is, however, no excuse for the head of music who fails to develop the band as a major contributing force in his school's activities. If he plays his essential part in this area of the school's music-making, the head of a music department can be of considerable assistance to the bandmaster. In too many schools failure to make proper links between the timetabled lessons and the special activities such as the choir, the orchestra, or the band, leads to failure in developing the maximum resources of a school.

The brass band has a most important role to play in a school's musical activities, and, together with a well developed ensemble organization of quartets, quintets, and so on, can provide a school with a most rewarding extension of its interests. One is constantly surprised at the rate at which a school can proceed in this direction. As an interesting example of the rapid establishment of a band, the following brief extract from an article may help to illustrate the sort of situation which often occurs:

> At the close of our first year we were a solid unit and playing confidently, having lost only half a dozen boys for various reasons. Their instruments, however, were immediately sought by new players on a long waiting list. We were also frequently reminded that the sooner we became expert on the instruments loaned, the more sympathetic would the Authority be in providing a new set... To me now a valve instrument ($B\flat$ and $E\flat$) has almost become a teach-yourself instrument for those with any ear at all for pitch, perhaps rivalling its counterpart the recorder for speed in learning and ultimate satisfaction. [1]

Such experiences have been repeated in many schools, and flourishing bands have been the result. It would be wrong, however, to overlook one important issue that is raised in this context: the do-it-yourself methods are all right as far as they go, but they also create very many difficulties for the player who really wishes to develop a good technique. Fundamental errors in sound production are very difficult to repair at a later stage, and (as is the case with the recorder) there is a vast difference between the ability to make a presentable noise in the cheerful club atmosphere of a band, and the ability to make an instrument sound at its best. There are, unfortunately, no short cuts in musical education.

The National School Brass Band Association has helped for the last twenty years or so to serve the needs of those involved in the development of bands in schools. It is therefore appropriate to conclude this chapter with some sensible

[1] Cole, H. E. 'Advent of Brass'; *Music in Education*, 32 (1968), p. 28.

remarks by Lance Caisley, who has been closely associated with the Association for many years:

> The school brass band is a necessary part of a full school musical education. It is not for everybody, any more than the school orchestra or the school choir is for everybody, but it ought to be there. As a complete and balanced combination it can more easily have a continuous life than any other instrumental group and it can be as easily integrated into the musical life of the school. The people who run our best school bands are complete musicians, as interested in Haydn's quartets, Walton's *Belshazzar's Feast*, or a Prokofiev symphony as in brass band music. For the school music teacher ought to have a catholic taste.[1]

[1] Caisley, L. 'Brass Bands in School'; *Sounding Brass*, 1 (1972), p. 23.

7 Brass in Your Orchestra

No doubt one of these days someone will come up with a detailed survey of the changes of emphasis in school music publishing which have taken place since the 1940s. In the meantime, however, a quick glance at the music cupboard of any long-established school reveals a great deal of information. There can be little doubt that in the early fifties publishers were still thinking in terms of string orchestras with a few optional wind parts. Quite often the arrangers seemed to have little idea of what to give the wind instruments, and from time to time trumpet parts in A or horn parts in G appeared. While young string players may be relatively happy in the keys of D and A, young trumpeters (with B♭ instruments) do not find comfort in E or B major. It is not, moreover, just a question of difficult transpositions. Sometimes the brass parts appear in impossible areas of the compass for young players to approach with any confidence.

Even if the brass parts are playable in some of the earlier publications, they are frequently very boring, and to deprive a young horn or trumpet player of the tune throughout a whole movement is unnecessarily thoughtless. Boredom also creeps into a rehearsal in which the brass players spend a considerable part of the time counting through empty bars waiting for their entry.

In recent years, however, there has been a growing realization on the part of the publishers that there are likely to be at least as many wind instruments as strings in school, and that scores intended for the school market must keep this constantly in mind. It is now possible to buy a wide range of works in which the brass instruments are given a fairly substantial role to play, and in which the scoring has taken into consideration the limitations of the instruments concerned without having to give them dull and uninteresting parts.

Clearly, where such scores also fulfil the more general musical requirements of the orchestra, they are preferable to the mainly string-conceived scores already referred to. Of course, for the more advanced orchestras the symphonic scores of the nineteenth and twentieth centuries often provide quite enough activity for the brass section. The first duty of the conductor in relation to the brass is to check that the parts are playable on the instruments available. It is most unlikely that many school players will have anything but a B flat trumpet or an F (or F/B♭) horn. While it is reasonable to expect players of about Grade 8 standard to be able to transpose at sight, less advanced performers will certainly require their parts to be in the conventional transpositions. Modern publications especially prepared for school use will naturally have the correct parts in the set, but often the well-known symphonic repertoire only exists in sets which contain the original transpositions. If a great deal of time is not to be wasted at rehearsal then it is essential that the new standard transpositions are prepared before the first rehearsal takes place.

Since it has been known for even the most experienced school conductors to get a little lost in the world of brass transpositions, let us just look at a typical problem. Here is the opening of Beethoven's Eighth Symphony:

The school certainly does not have trumpets in F, so the part must be played on B♭ instruments. What is the actual sound intended? In Beethoven's time the trumpet with an F-crook produced notes a perfect fourth higher than the written notes, so the actual sound would have been

For a B♭ instrument today the part would have to be written as follows:

The actual part throughout the symphony is easy, but without a newly written-out transposition, many young players would be confronted by totally unnecessary difficulties.

Having satisfied himself that the parts are correct, the next requirement is for the conductor to plan rehearsals so that the brass players are usefully employed. Again, taking the Eighth Symphony as an example, the trumpets are not required at all in the second movement or in the Trio of the third movement, and so these sections might either be taken during the second half of a rehearsal or at a complete rehearsal without trumpets. On such an occasion the trumpets can be rehearsed with the trombones and tuba in a separate section rehearsal of a work for full orchestra. The conductor also must realize that most brass players need something of a warm-up before they can get the best out of their instruments, and that a little preliminary exercise for them willl make the rehearsal get off to a good start. It need hardly be added that long sustained passages in the high register make considerable demands upon even the most accomplished players, and that too many attempts at a high difficult passage are likely to be self-defeating.

Most brass players find it difficult to behave like those other instrumentalists who are able to go through their parts at a final rehearsal with reduced dynamics. This point is well illustrated by Denis Wick when he writes that 'Conductors have often complained that the brass section is playing too strongly at a final rehearsal. What usually happens is that the strings and woodwind of a symphony orchestra tend to take it easy at such a rehearsal. They have a fairly continuous effort to make and need to conserve their strength and energy. While this can also apply to the brass, they have a special need to play in exactly the same way as they do in performance so that phrasing, breathing, and lip-control can be arranged properly. These same conductors who complain of too much volume at the dress rehearsal also call for more and more sound at the performance.'[1]

It is usual to place the brass section of an orchestra right at the back of the platform, and it is therefore important that the conductor ensures that his signals to them are absolutely clear from a distance. A very low or indecisive beat can cause chaos in this department and stray brass entries are the last thing a conductor wants. Inexperienced players will often have difficulties with their lowest notes, and fail to make them 'speak' right on the beat. If they can become accustomed to a steady and clear beat from the conductor they can often overcome this difficulty by slightly anticipating the beat.

Perhaps the last point that the non-wind-playing conductor needs to remember in his treatment of young wind players is the obvious matter of the players' health. Brass players with a cold, or sore lips, or teeth problems cannot perform properly. The clarity of their playing may disappear altogether, and the obtaining of notes from the higher harmonics may become just a matter of chance. Even the best horn players 'crack' their top notes from time to time, and sustained high passages on the trumpet or the trombone also need very controlled lip

[1] Denis Wick, *Trombone Technique* (O.U.P. 1971), p. 111.

movements on the part of the players. When they are physic-
ally below their best, the difficulties are considerably increased.

The role of brass in the Wind Orchestra is so completely
covered in the companion volume to this book, Sidney
Lawton's *The Wind Orchestra* (in preparation), that the reader
is referred to that source for specialist information.

8 Brass with Your Choir

Now that school choirs have become much more interested in performing the fine choral works of the late renaissance, it is not surprising that many conductors have looked towards the brass players in the school to provide the appropriate accompaniments. A brass ensemble has at least two major advantages over the organ as the instrumental accompaniment in such music: the organ is, as often as not, only to be found in the local church, which means that the choir has no choice but to rehearse and perform there, whereas the brass ensemble can play anywhere. Secondly, the brass ensemble enables the school to provide their own instrumental accompaniment for the choir, and thus expands the players' experience of music beyond the purely instrumental.

A choir of about forty singers needs no more than a quartet or quintet to take the instrumental parts, while a larger choir hardly ever needs more than ten to twelve players. The rich sonorities that are possible in these contexts seem to draw out the best from both singers and players. Most of the major publishers have a few items on their lists for choir and brass including some recent works by modern composers; but there is still a vast field to explore.

The late renaissance motet is a particularly suitable vehicle for experiments with brass and choral sonorities, for it must be remembered that the style of writing that Gabrieli, for example, employs in many of his canzonas differs only marginally from his vocal style. The whole Italian field provides literally hundreds of pieces that could justly be called 'apt for voices or brass', and the English madrigal school also lends itself to interesting possibilities. Of course, the playing of linear counterpoint introduces the young brass player to problems of phrasing and accentuation which he does not often encounter elsewhere, and conductors may have to spend some time in developing the appropriate style of playing. Nevertheless, such experience is of considerable importance to the young musician, and the brass/choir motet provides an obvious extension to the canzona experience which the player should be getting in the purely instrumental field.

Antiphonal music for two, three, or more choirs provides marvellous opportunities for the use of brass. George Draper has successfully arranged Gabrieli's *O magnum mysterium* for two brass choirs (published by O.U.P.), but such a work also lends itself to voices/choir 1 and brass/choir 2, particularly if a proper space is allowed between the positions of the two groups. If a choir does not have the resources to split up into two, three, or more smaller choirs, then the brass ensemble can simply take over the music of one or more of the groups. Some of the American publishers have gone further in this direction than their British counterparts, but there are sufficient examples now available for the enthusiastic conductor to develop his interests in a number of directions.

The following list may indicate some of the possibilities in the chorus and brass field:

Barber, S., *Easter chorale*, for chorus, brass, timpani, and organ (Chappell)

Bieske, W., *Vater unser im Himmelreich*, for chorus and brass (Bärenreiter)

Bruckner, A., *Two motets*, for chorus and 3 trombones (Hinrichsen)

Brugk, H. M., *Bläser-Messe*, for chorus and brass (Schott)

Copley, I., *The trumpet carol*, for mixed voices and 3 trumpets (Thames)

Cruft, A., *Benedictus*, for chorus & brass ensemble (Boosey & Hawkes)

Cruft, A., *Jubilate Deo*, for chorus & brass ensemble (Boosey & Hawkes)

Fortig, P., *Ave verum corpus*, for chorus & brass octet (Bärenreiter)

Gabrieli, G., *In ecclesiis*, for double chorus, 3 trumpets, 3 trombones, and organ (Schirmer)

Gabrieli, G., *Jubilate Deo*, for chorus, 4 trumpets, & 4 trombones (Schirmer)

Harrison, L., *Processionals*, for chorus, trombone ensemble, and percussion (Hinrichsen)

Hindemith, P., *Apparebit repentina dies*, for chorus & brass (Schott)

Hovhaness, A., *Glory to God*, for soprano & alto soloists, chorus, brass, percussion, & organ (Hinrichsen)

Koch, J. H. E., *Gottes Sohn ist gekommen*, for chorus & brass (Bärenreiter)

Koch, J. H. E., *Komm, heiliger Geist, herre Gott*, for chorus & brass (Bärenreiter)

Koch, J. H. E., *Dann wachet*, for soprano & alto soloists, chorus, & trombone ensemble (Bärenreiter)

Layton, B. J., *Three Dylan Thomas poems*, for chorus & brass sextet (Schirmer)

Lewkovich, B., *Veni creator Spiritus*, for chorus & 6 trombones (Chester)

McCabe, J., *Great Lord of Lords*, for chorus, brass, organ, & timpani (Novello)

Mellers, W., *Two motets*, for chorus, 2 trumpets, 4 horns, & 3 trombones (O.U.P.)

Rein, W., *Zu Bethlehem geboren*; carol for chorus & brass (Bärenreiter)

Schuemann, B., *Das Gleichnis von Unkraut unter dem Weizen*, for chorus, 2 trumpets, & 2 trombones (Bärenreiter)

Schütz, H., *Die mit Tränen säen*, motet for 2 five-part choirs with 6 trombones and continuo (Bärenreiter)

Schütz, H., *Ist nicht Ephraim mein teurer Sohn?*; motet for chorus and brass octet (O.U.P.)

Schütz, H., *Psalm 8*, for chorus & brass (Bärenreiter)

Vaughan Williams, R., *The Old Hundredth*, arr. for choir, 3 trumpets, & organ (O.U.P.)

Wenzel, E., *Gott des Himmels und der Erden*, for chorus & brass (Bärenreiter)

$\mathcal{9}$ Developing a Library

Time spent in organizing a library of scores and parts is well spent, not only for materials in the brass repertoire, but for all branches of the school's musical activities. It is not an aspect of school life that can be taken lightly, for the high price of printed music makes it essential that once a set of parts is bought, it remains available for performance for many years.

No doubt every school will develop its own system, but the following points need to be kept in mind:

Cataloguing
A card index is the most useful, with composer, title, and each instrument for which there is a part listed. For cross-reference an entry should also be made on a separate card, with one for quartets, another for quintets, and so on. Each work needs a catalogue number.

Shelving
Scores and parts come in various sizes, and the easiest way of storing them is in a standard folder, on the inside cover of which the complete list of parts is given. Where the publisher has provided alternative sets of parts, these should be listed as substitutions for each instrument. It is only too easy to misplace the alternative second horn part one year when it is not being used, only to find you need it the next. When someone has taken the trouble to write out a complete transposition of a part, it should be preserved for another occasion and entered on the list of instruments in the folder.

Checking in and out
When a set of parts is finished with for the present, a thorough check should be made that every part has been handed in. A member of the ensemble/band/orchestra is usually willing to act as librarian. Each school will have to develop a clearly defined policy towards the lending of parts: either to lend out the parts so that they can be practised, but possibly forgotten for the next rehearsal; or to collect them after every rehearsal so that they are always available for group rehearsal but not for private practice. The long-term answer is always to have two sets of parts.

Borrowing from outside
No school can afford to buy all the music it needs, and it is therefore important that a member of the staff has access to the resources of the local education authority and the public library system. Theoretically there is no published music that cannot be borrowed from somewhere, provided one tries hard enough. Of course especial care needs to be taken of borrowed music, and conductors must restrain themselves from telling their players to mark their parts with new phrasing, dynamics, cuts, and repeats. Most local authorities who employ a music adviser also equip him with a central music collection, and an up-to-date list of what is available should be in every school. As when using the professional hire libraries, it is as well to plan well in advance: a well organized department will always plan its concerts one or two terms in advance, and even this may not be enough time unless the programme contains several options.

Purchasing
Most publishers operate some type of inspection system, and teachers are advised to take advantage of this whenever possible. Within the week or so that they can inspect the

scores, most teachers will be able to form an impression of whether or not the publications fit their requirements. The head of a music department should in any case be on the mailing list of all the major publishing houses, and armed with these catalogues, and a regular copy of one of the music education periodicals, he should have no difficulty in keeping up with current trends. American teachers are fortunate in having regularly revised surveys like *Brass Players' Guide to the Literature* (compiled by Robert Corley)[1] but in this country there is no exact equivalent. It is hoped, however, that the catalogue at the end of this book will prove a useful step in that direction.

[1] Published by the Robert King Company, North Easton, Massachusetts, USA.

10 Instrumental Tuition

Although in a few schools the teaching of brass instruments will be carried out by a member of the full-time staff, in the majority of cases it will be members of the part-time visiting staff who take on the responsibility. Relationships between full- and part-time members of staff are extremely variable. In some schools the peripatetic staff are fully drawn into the school's music programme, and discuss with the head of department not only the individual progress of pupils, but also the best ways of encouraging the young player to take his place in ensembles, bands, and orchestras. For such teachers, time-tables are properly organized, rooms appropriately equipped, copies adequately supplied, instruments made available, and personal problems discussed.

In other schools, chilling tales of non-existent accommodation, poor facilities, erratic timetables, failures in communication, and fundamentally no sense of structure or purpose in the teaching programme can only be believed because they occur so frequently. If the visiting teacher is to make a worthwhile contribution to the musical education of a school his work must obviously be seen as part of the whole, and what he does must be seen to affect whatever else is going on.

The brass teacher needs a reasonable-sized room in which to teach, for he cannot teach good sound production in a box. He needs music stands, storage space for instruments, books, and sheet music; a good tape recorder is also a valuable asset and should be available. It must not be forgotten that he may well spend as much as one or two days in a school in each week, and that he needs the same comforts as any other teacher. One cannot really expect very good teaching from teachers who are asked to put up with medical rooms, cupboards, assembly halls, and even corridors.

Timetable policy must be in the hands of the school, but many visiting teachers have experience of working in a wide variety of conditions and can probably give advice on which systems work better than others. Most schools will insist upon some sort of rotating timetable so that different 'normal' lessons are missed each week. However, such timetables need constant attention from the permanent and visiting staff. A substitute system is also highly desirable, for the time of a visiting specialist is valuable, and sitting about waiting for pupils who are absent from school is understandably unpopular. The head of a large department may well have ten or more regular peripatetic staff teaching in his school. However hard pressed he is with his own teaching and concert activity, time spent in making smooth arrangements for them is time well spent.

One of the major problems that a school has to face in the context of brass teaching is whether to have the bandmaster type of teacher, who can put his hand to any brass instrument, or specialists in trumpet, horn, and trombone. There is no doubt that the good bandmaster is a very great asset to a school, and he certainly suits the L.E.A., which in any case finds great difficulty in appointing the right sort of staff. Such a person appears to be able to cope with every candidate from soprano cornet to bass tuba, and is therefore able to fit into practically any teaching requirement.

The accomplished bandmaster, who in any case is not as common as one would like, would, however, be the first to agree that there are as many differences in technique demanded by brass instruments as there are in the woodwind sector. If a young horn player, for example, begins his lessons with a teacher who is essentially a trumpeter, fundamental problems of embouchure may never be solved. One uses the word *may*, for it is not an absolute rule, and there are many good teachers who can teach on instruments as different as the french horn and the trombone. Nevertheless, the advantages of employing specialists from the first lesson seem, to many people, to outweigh the inevitable organizational problems.

Such specialist teaching is often to be found in the area music centre, to which students can be sent instead of receiving lessons in their own school. The advantages of such a system are considerable, for a centralized institution is usually better equipped and better staffed, and the possibilities of orchestral activity on a large scale exist at a very much higher level. At the same time, the loss to the school as a community can often be very damaging indeed. If most of the young players become accustomed to going off to the local centre for their musical activities, it is difficult to persuade them that they also have a responsibility towards their own school. This may not matter to them, but it certainly does matter to the rest of the school who may, in effect, be deprived of their contribution to the well-being of the school.

The best music centres can, and often do, make excellent provision for the young player. In a city environment such a centre is never too far away. In rural areas, however, long journeys are often undertaken by parents willing to take advantage of what is offered. Possibly one of the greatest advantages of the centralized form of teaching is that a certain continuity of teaching can be provided, and the divisions between primary, middle, and secondary schools, which can so easily interrupt the natural development of a child's instrumental skills, can be avoided.

Weekly lessons, of course, are of no value unless they are accompanied by a week's practice. Now while the majority of schools can provide regular teaching, few of them attempt to provide facilities for practice. In the view of many people associated with musical education the school has a definite responsibility towards providing such facilities, for the accommodation problems of many families make it almost impossible for a child to practice an instrument at home.

After-school provision of rooms, however, is not enough. Children in school must in any case be supervised, and supervision by a musician is really what is required in this context, for many young players really do need help in between their weekly lessons. Moreover, when pianists are available, this does provide them with an opportunity to practice pieces that demand an accompaniment.

Brass specialist teachers will need no advice on the maintenance of instruments for they are only too familiar with the problems of bent slides, sticking valves, and clogged-up mouthpieces. For the all-round teacher, however, it is perhaps appropriate to mention three points: first, it should be remembered that brass instruments always need lubrication and that therefore the safest thing to do is for the teacher to provide valve and slide oil at all rehearsals, so that players who have forgotten to bring their own can at least have a working instrument throughout a rehearsal or performance; second, that young players should be constantly reminded about cleaning their instruments, just as they need reminding about washing behind their ears; third, that no major engineering should be attempted by amateurs – it will be much cheaper in the long run to have repairs carried out by skilled craftsmen.

Some teachers of brass like to see their pupils making visible progress by entering them for examinations at regular intervals, while others find such a way of working uncongenial. It is desirable, however, for the school to form a known policy on such matters, and if examinations are part of such a policy, the permanent staff of the school should take a full part in the process. Most practical examinations demand accompanied pieces, and the school should make a point of introducing the young player to a regular accompanist well before the examination itself. One can only pity the pupil who meets his accompanist (and sometimes *any* accompanist) for the first time at the actual examination. Again, most examinations demand aural tests which can certainly be prepared by the class teacher. Finally, someone should check that the right scales and arpeggios, and the right level of sight reading, are being practised, for it is, in the end, the responsibility of the head of the music department to ensure that the appropriate syllabuses have been followed. In the limited time at his disposal the brass teacher ought to be able to concentrate on matters of technique and interpretation, and not on matters which can be adequately assigned to others.

Appendix: The Canzonas of Giovanni Gabrieli

Giovanni Gabrieli's published instrumental ensemble works nominally amount to forty-two, and were published in three groups: sixteen among the vocal works of the *Sacrae symphoniae* in 1597; six in a collection of works by several composers published in Venice in 1608 by Alessandro Raverio, entitled *Canzoni per sonare*; and twenty in *Canzoni e sonate*, published by G. Magni in Venice in 1615, that is, three years after the composer's death. There are, however, really only forty different works: the 1597 collection contains two versions of the *Canzon duodecimi toni*, one for double five-part groups, and one for double five-part groups with organs, described by Gabrieli as *Canzon in echo*. The second duplication occurs when the same eight-part work appears as *Canzon 27* in the 1608 collection, and *Canzon 9* in the 1615 collection.

The publications are by no means in chronological order of composition, and some of the earliest examples appear in the 1608 set. The instrumentation was generally not specified. The resources involved range from four parts to twenty-two parts, with the majority of the works demanding from eight to twelve players. No special significance can be attached to the term 'sonata', which is given to several of the canzonas.

All forty works can be performed by trumpets and trombones only, and there can be no doubt that these instruments are particularly suited to the performance of both complex contrapuntal textures and broad harmonic passages. However, demands for up to seventeen trombones (1615, no.20) are very likely to meet with some astonishment, and most schools will have to deploy their forces in whatever way seems most appropriate. Advice on the scoring of each work occurs in the notes which follow. It must be remembered (see p. 15) that the many tenor-clef trombone parts can easily be read by treble-clef B flat transposing instruments (e.g. treble-clef trombone readers, baritones, and euphoniums). Tubas in F and E flat can, of course, replace some of the trombone parts, thus releasing them to play tenor parts, but the BB♭ tuba can usually only be used for sub-octave doubling in large groups.

All modern performing editions of the works of Gabrieli and his contemporaries introduce bar lines. The obvious convenience which they provide may turn into a severe disadvantage if the bar lines are seen in terms of heavy first-beat accents. In every canzona the players will encounter examples in which the point of entry of a motif within the bar may vary without the accentuation of the motif itself requiring any alteration, e.g.

and

Players who are not accustomed to this sense of rhythm must be restrained from banging down powerful accents in inappropriate places. It may prove necessary in rehearsal to ask all the players to run through the first entry version of all the thematic material so that they can all fully appreciate the nature of the phrasing required for the appropriate performance of such music.

Most of the pieces contain alternating sections in duple (or quadruple) and triple time. The standard procedures are:

or $\qquad \frac{2}{2}\left(\frac{4}{4}\right)\mathbf{o} \qquad = \qquad \frac{3}{4}\; \raisebox{-0.3ex}{$\downarrow$}\!.$

depending upon the note values employed. In general, then, the effect is one of regulated twos and threes, but conductors should not feel obliged to get out their metronomes in order to produce *exact* relationships. It should be remembered that these works often contain a wide variety of note values, and that it is important to set the overall tempo at a pace which allows the players to cope with the semiquaver and demi-semiquaver passages. N.B. Many modern editors halve the original note values, so that minim becomes crotchet, and so on.

The following performing notes on the forty canzonas are divided into eight groups: quartets, quintets, sextets, septets, octets, 10-part, 12-part, and 14 or more parts. The abbreviations used are: Tr = trumpet; Tb = trombone; Hn = Horn in F; Ct = cornet; E♭ Hn = Tenor Horn; Bar = Baritone Horn; Euph = Euphonium; Tba = Tuba. Brackets indicate alternatives.

QUARTETS

There are four canzonas for four instruments, and they are all to be found in the 1608 publication. They can be performed by the following instruments:

(i) Tr I II Tb I (Hn) II
(ii) Ct I II E♭Hn Bar (Euph)

The best performances of these quartets on modern brass instruments are usually achieved by two trumpets and two trombones. There can be little doubt that the more incisive tone of the trombone is generally to be preferred to that of the French horn (or indeed the E flat horn) in the tenor part, for in the contrapuntal passages the horn can easily be obscured. At the same time, one would not hesitate to recommend any combination of instruments that allowed young players to experience the rewards of playing this splendid music.

The quartets make an excellent introduction to Gabrieli's instrumental style, combining elements of simple contrapuntal and bold harmonic textures. For groups new to the style, probably the order of approach should be 1, 4, 3, and 2. (There are some easy pieces among the double quartets.)

Quartet no. 1
Canzon I (1608) 'La Spiritata'
Tr I II Tb I (Hn) II

This delightful and relatively easy canzona should never sound too hurried, particularly in the last section (bars 63—end)[1] where the semiquaver entries can easily become ragged. The opening four bars for trumpets are answered by the lower instruments, and it is important that the full value of notes at the end of phrases should be demanded, so that the transition from one voice to another is achieved without loss of continuity or balance. Make sure that the change from 2/2 to 3/4 is smooth. The close entries of the section 36—44 need careful rehearsal with very tidy rhythmic playing to ensure a translucent texture, as also does the more difficult final section.

---

[1] The numbering of works, and references to bar numbers, are according to the editions published by Musica Rara (see pp. 112—14).

Quartet no. 2
Canzon II (1608)
Tr I II Tb I (Hn) II

The second four-part canzona is an altogether more brilliant piece than the first. In setting the pace it is important to check that the trombones can play the trumpets' initial phrase without sounding too hurried. The second quaver entries for each instrument in bars 20–32 need to be rhythmically precise, and the four-part chords at 32–35 absolutely together. The middle part of the canzona can afford to be fairly relaxed in order to constrast with the return of the first idea at bars 73ff. The final section should be played with as much brilliance as can be produced without straining the players.

This work has striking similarities with the third canzona, which is in many ways easier to perform and might profitably be explored before No. 2.

Quartet no. 3
Canzon III (1608)
Tr I II Tb I (Hn) II

The third quartet has many points of similarity with No. 2 but is, in some respects, easier to play, especially as the quaver passages are much shorter. Unlike No. 2, however, there is a change to triple time for a short section, and this must be approached and quitted without interruption in the flow of the music. As in the first canzona, a regular crotchet beat is, on the whole desirable, but some conductors may prefer to take the triple-time section at a more leisurely pace.

Bars 15—39 of No. 3 should be compared with bars 20—32 of No. 2, as both these sections demand very clean entries. The chordal passage 49—53, though simple enough, demands very precise articulation to achieve the appropriate effect. The return of the first subject (bars 62ff.) should be carried off with great brilliance, and without loss of pace.

Quartet no. 4

Tr I II Tb I (Hn) II

Although this quartet is quite straightforward in many respects, there are one or two passages which tend to expose weak players, and must therefore be handled with very great care, e.g. the first trumpet part at bars 12—15, 32—35, 74—76, and the second trumpet at 22—26. Some of the second trumpet passages lie rather low, and it is essential that the proper balance between the parts be achieved at such points. (If a good horn player is available there is something to be said for performing this quartet with Tr, Hn, Tb I, Tb II.) The section bars 50—62 is simple but effective, and makes an excellent preparation for the return of the main subject at bar 63.

QUINTET

There is only one quintet in the Gabrieli collection, and so groups of this size must look elsewhere for further examples in this style, e.g. Pezel, Franck, Holborne, Schein, et al.

Canzon I (1615)
(i) Tr I II Hn(Tb)Tb I II
(ii) Ct I Ct II E♭ Hn Euph I Euph II (Bar)

For rehearsal purposes this piece may be divided into four sections, viz. bars 1—30, bars 30—40, bars 40—48, bars 48—end. The first section provides a complete working-out of the main subject, and clear-cut rhythms and clean lines are essential if the five-part counterpoint is to be shown to its best effect. It is, of course, essential to see that all the players adopt the same phrasing, and that they listen to each other as they play. Above all, any attempts to place heavy accents on all first beats of the bar, regardless of their relative position within the phrase, will create very ugly playing. Remember that the bar lines are there only for our convenience. E.g.

The second section demands great rhythmic precision, and very clear articulation on the dotted rhythms. The third section, with its open textures, can easily come to grief in the hands of inexperienced players, and may require extra rehearsal. The return of the main idea at bar 48 leads to a triumphant conclusion.

SEXTETS

Perhaps the first thing to be said about the three superb sextets is that players should not allow themselves to be frightened by the demisemiquaver passages that occur in the concluding sections of each of these works. They are little more than ornamental, and provided that a sensible tempo is set, which allows the players to articulate the semiquaver passages without undue haste, these examples of early baroque decoration will drop into the general scheme of things without too much trouble. Probably a tempo of ♩ = 60−66 will be fast enough.

The second general point concerns instrumentation: each of the three works demands a different combination of instruments, so that they cannot be played as a group of pieces by the same players. However, the standard two trumpet/two trombone quartet can invite guest appearances from among their friends.

Sextet no. 1
Canzon II (1615)
Tr I II III Tb I (Hn) Tb II Tb III

Unlike the quartets and quintet, this canzona is less obviously divided into sections. The first motif and the counter-subject $\left(\flat \ \text{♩. ♩ ♩. ♩ ♩} \ _{etc.} \right)$ occupy all the players almost exclusively until bar 30. This first section shows a complete working-out of the principal ideas, and the six-part texture provides many opportunities for Gabrieli to demonstrate his fluent contrapuntal technique. Notice that Trumpets

I and II are equals, each taking the top line in turn, so it is important to listen for the proper balance between parts.

Bars 31—36 need careful handling if the thinner texture of this section is not to sound weak. The return at bar 36 of the main subject also brings with it some extended passage work for several of the players which may require special attention. The trumpet flourishes at bar 57 are no more than a succession of turns, and lead to a short section in triple time, which should involve few difficulties, if the players are encouraged to aim for continuity. The last section is a coda with elaborate trumpet decorations which, if necessary, should be simplified, provided always that the harmonic structure is preserved.

Sextet no. 2
Canzon III (1615)
Tr I II Hn (Tr III/Tb) Tb I (Hn) II III*(Tba)
*B♭/F trombone required

As in the first sextet, there is only a short contrasting section in triple time, and a highly decorative coda (which need not cause any major difficulties, provided that a reasonably steady tempo is established).

The first section (bars 1—16) requires the usual clarity of texture, and special attention must be made to ensure that the two middle parts come through properly.

At bar 17 the metre in effect becomes 3+3+2 for a few moments, but it would be a mistake to force the accents. The triple-time section (bars 25—34), with its simple texture and rhythms, should form a complete contrast to preceding material, without, however, any break in the music. This triple section in turn gives way to the part of the canzona which may provide the most difficulties: the counterpoint in the passage bars 35—47 requires a very keen sense of line and texture from the players, and the rhythm of bars 51—54 may cause some bother if the players do not grasp the internal patterns within the four beats. The dotted rhythms that lead to the final flourish should be played with absolute precision.

Sextet no. 3
Canzon IV (1615)
Tr I II III IV Tb I II

The brilliant third sextet is unlike any of the preceding works, consisting of alternating four- and three-beat sections (4-3-4-3-4-3-4-3-4), in which the triple-time sections take the form of a simple dance-like homophony, in response to the counterpoint of the four-beat sections.

Only three instruments have had time to bring in the main idea before the first interruption takes place. These kaleidoscopic changes of rhythm and texture demand very sensitive playing from the instrumentalists, and considerable flexibility in the higher registers from the first and second trumpets.

The first major problem is deciding on the relative paces of the contrasting sections. The semiquavers of the first section must not be too rushed, but neither must the crotchets of the $\frac{3}{4}$ be too laboured: $\frac{4}{4} \, \downarrow = \frac{3}{4} \, \downarrow .$ is generally acceptable. The final coda, with its bold harmonies, is a glorious opportunity for display.

SEPTETS

The three seven-part canzonas can be played by the same combination of instruments

e.g. (i) Tr I II III IV* Tb I (Tr V/Hn) II III
      (ii) Ct I II III IV* E♭Hn Euph Tb
      (*This part might suit a *good* horn (F or E♭) player)

They are full of marvellous kaleidoscopic changes of texture and, apart from the last section of No. 3, are relatively easy to perform.

Septet no. 1
Canzon V (1615)
Tr I II III IV* Tb I (Tr V/Hn) II III
(*Tr IV might be played by a good horn player)

For rehearsal purposes the work may be divided into the following sections: 1−10, 10−17, 17−38, 38−52, 52−end.

Throughout the work the bass line is shared by Trombones II and III, so it is important to ensure that these parts are well balanced. A steady pace for the opening will allow the subsequent semiquaver passages to flow along without undue haste. Considerable attention should be paid to the rests in each part, so that plenty of daylight gets into the elaborate contrapuntal texture. Clear articulation and light playing without vibrato will lead to the best sound. The second section demands very accurate rhythmic pointing if it is not to sound untidy. The third section contains some problems of balance and the approach to, and quitting of, the triple-time section. In the fourth section, which leads back to the original tonic, the semiquaver runs should be played as lightly as possible in order not to obscure the return of the original motiv. The final section, as usual, provides a splendid climax.

Septet no. 2
Canzon VI (1615)
Tr I II III IV Tb I (Hn) II III

Although this is not a difficult piece as far as the individual instruments are concerned, there are problems to be overcome in the constantly changing textures. Sustained passages of seven-part writing are comparatively rare, and there is a constant regrouping of antiphonal sections in which two, three, or four instruments are answered by another group. This type of music can only successfully be played by instrumentalists who listen to each other with the very closest attention, and who can hear the melodic ideas being passed around from instrument to instrument. Some of the best playing will come from groups which have also had some experience of singing madrigals, for it is a light madrigal style that is most appropriate to this canzona.

Septet no. 3
Canzon VII (1615)
Tr I II III IV Tb I (Hn) II III

This is one of the few examples of a long opening section in what is mainly $\frac{6}{8}$ rhythm with a few $\frac{3}{4}$ endings to the phrases. As in the second septet, there are relatively few places when all seven instruments are playing at once, and Gabrieli's main achievement lies in the wonderfully delicate changes of texture that characterize these works. The playing must therefore be dance-like, with buoyant rhythms and clearly moulded phrases. It would be unwise, however, to allow the opening section to rush away with itself, for the elaboration to come in the section bars 115−132 must be borne in mind from the start, recognizing that a bar of $\frac{6}{8}$ will equal half a bar of $\frac{4}{4}$, and

that he who plays ♩ ♪ ♩ ♪ must be able to play

♫♫♫ ♫♫♫ ♫♫♫ ♫♫♫ in the same length of time.

OCTETS

All except one of the thirteen eight-part canzonas are for double-choir performance and there is, therefore, a need to attempt some sort of balance between the two groups. From the very first rehearsal the players should become accustomed to the spatial significance of the music, and should learn to listen to the way the music passes from one area to another without interruption. Where possible, a gap of several yards should occur between the two groups so that the identity of each group can really be felt by the players.

With one or two exceptions it is possible to think of these works in terms of double quartets, and thus the following groups can tackle most of the material:

(i) Tr I II Tb I (Hn) II
(ii) Ct I II E♭Hn Bar/Euph

However, Gabrieli is very interested in a wide range of features, and the instrumentation for each canzona should be carefully examined to find the best solution.

Octet no. 1
Canzon Primi Toni (1597)
Choir 1: Tr I II Tb I (Hn/Tr) II
Choir 2: Tr I II Tb I (Hn/Tr) II

The opening eight bars of choir 1 are immediately echoed by choir 2 so it is important to establish from the start a common approach to the phrasing. Set a pace in which the later semiquavers can be played with comfort. In the ensuing imitative passage allow each of the rapid close entries to sound clearly, and ensure that the inner counterpoint is not swamped by the first trumpet. It is also essential that, when the real bass line passes from one choir to the other, there is not a sudden change in weight (e.g. bars 19–20). The section bars 1–24 is repeated 24–47: consider what dynamic changes might be introduced to advantage. The changes to triple metre should be accomplished without any interruption to the flow of the music. Some conductors may wish to employ a slight relaxation of tempo in the last section in order to give more weight to the climax, but this should not begin until bar 132.

Octet no. 2
Canzon Septimi Toni No. 1 (1597)
Choir 1: Tr I II Tb I (Hn/Tr) II
Choir 2: Tr I II Tb I (Hn/Tr) II

The fugal entries of the first choir may lead to an uncertain beginning unless a strict tempo is maintained from the very first beat. A *forte* is probably also required in order to provide firmness of texture. The second choir's entry is not a repeat, and the music must flow from one choir to the other without break. The other instruments must be encouraged to play their quaver passages as lightly as the trumpets. The second choir passage bars 62—77 is probably the most difficult section to bring off effectively, and a good deal of encouragement may be required in getting the details right. In the echo sections of the triple-time music, make sure that the entries are exactly on the beat, and that the full value of the notes at the ends of phrases is secured. The magnificent climax of the last section should not lead the performers to lose sight of the intricate counterpoint in eight parts that concludes the canzona.

Octet no. 3
Canzon Septimi Toni No. 2
Choir 1: Tr I II Tb I (Hn/Tr) II
Choir 2: Tr I II Tb I (Hn/Tr) II

This canzona is mainly written in a simple homophonic style, with the two choirs imitating each other in bright splashes of sound. For this reason it makes a most attractive work for beginners in the double-quartet field, and provided that the main principles of Gabrieli's style are kept in mind (e.g. playing right through the phrases in all parts, avoiding over-emphasis on first beats, relaxing the ends of phrases except at the final cadence, dovetailing the entries of the antiphonal groups) it is a work that should meet with a great deal of success. It is tempting to rush away with the opening crotchets, but the quavers of bar 7 *et seq.* should be allowed to set the overall pace. The changes from four to three beats and back again should provide few difficulties provided that the music is allowed to flow onwards. (The first choir is generally given the responsibility for establishing the new rhythm, so it might be better to place the more experienced players in this group).

Octet no. 4
Canzon Noni Toni (1597)
Choir 1: Tr I II Tb I (Hn/Tr) II
Choir 2: Tr I II Tb I (Hn/Tr) II

The fourth of the octets has much in common with the second, starting with a fugal-style opening for the first choir. However, once the second choir has entered, the style becomes much more homophonic, and the usual double-choir techniques of imitation are used with their customary effectiveness. Make sure that each of the entries is firm, and that the notes are given their full values in order to avoid patchiness in the texture. Throughout the canzona, both in the duple and triple sections it is vital that the rhythms are given plenty of spring and bounce, to encourage the players to lean towards a light dance-like sound, reserving their really broad tone for the final six bars. The constant passing of the music from one group to another is easy enough once the players have become accustomed to listening to each other all the time, and imitating each other's phrasing.

Octet no. 5
Canzon Duodecimi Toni (1597)
Choir 1: Tr I II Tb I (Hn/Tr) II
Choir 2: Tr I II Tb I (Hn/Tr) II

This canzona has much in common with No. 4, employing a similar opening motif, and using the same techniques of imitation and structure. However, players who know both works will find a lot of pleasure in discovering the variety of techniques that Gabrieli employs with such apparent freedom. The longer notes in the section bars 26—36 provide the players with an opportunity to produce some rich sonorities, and the conductor must listen very carefully for a real balance of parts. If trombones are used for the tenor parts they must not be allowed to force their tone too much on the higher notes and thus spoil the even textures that are demanded in such passages. The canonic writing for the two bass parts (63—74) must be well articulated, and any attempt to swamp the other parts must be resisted. The fifth canzona is somewhat longer than its predecessor, and the players will need plenty of energy to bring off the final section with maximum effect.

Octet no. 6
Sonata Pian' e Forte
Choir 1: Tr I II (Hn) Tb I (Hn/Tr) II
Choir 2: Tb I (Hn) II III IV (Tba)

This canzona is the last of the 1597 octets and, unlike the other five, is written for two contrasting groups (not, it should be noted, for one *piano* group, and one *forte* group). The first choir is the normal quartet (although the second trumpet part is on the low side, and could be replaced by a horn or another trombone if one is available). The second quartet can be played entirely by trombones, although the obvious substitutions of horns and/or euphoniums are possible. This work has long been the introduction to Gabrieli's music for many players, and the mere possession of a famous title has had the inevitable attracting force. It must be pointed out, however, that it is a most unsuitable work for beginners in a number of ways. First, the absence of the usual quota of trumpets tends to make a rather sombre sound, and, as there are usually quite a lot of trumpet players about in any case, a work which excludes them is not a very suitable choice; second, the attention to problems of dynamic contrast often tends to lead to the neglect of the basic stylistic requirements that all Gabrieli's music demands, i.e. correct phrasing, balancing textures, clear melodic lines, pointed rhythms, etc.; third, as a canzona in eight parts it presents a number of tricky points which are not found in the easier, and possibly more rewarding, Nos. 3 and 5, for example.

Nevertheless, for a group with plenty of trombone and/or horn players, this is a work that will provide a good deal of satisfaction. They must learn to approach it with the same dance-like rhythms that are found in all the other canzonas. The actual areas of dynamic contrast may suggest a similar approach to some of the other canzonas.

(See also Octets 9 and 12 for similar instrumentation.)

Octet no. 7
Canzon XXVII (1608)/Canzon IX (1615)
Tr I II III Hn I (Tr/Tb) II (Tb) Tb I II III

This is the only one of the eight-part canzonas that is not written on the double-quartet principle, and so it should be compared more with the style of writing encountered in the septets than with the other octets. It makes a very interesting work to study in relationship to the third septet (Canzon VII, 1615), in which the extended $\frac{6}{8}$ section only gives way to the $\frac{4}{4}$ in the final section. In this octet, the long $\frac{3}{4}$ section (with $\frac{6}{8}$ cross-rhythms) only leaves space for ten bars of $\frac{4}{4}$ at the conclusion, and even this is interrupted by the incessant dance rhythms of the main material. A great variety of textures is produced, but as with the septets, there are relatively few moments in which all eight instruments are sounding. Passages in thirds crop up all over the score with different pairs of instruments, and ensemble playing of a very high order is constantly demanded.

For rehearsal purposes the work might be divided into the following sections: 1–12, 13–38, 38–56, 56–71, 71–100, and 100–end. None of the parts is individually very difficult, and the bass part is very simple indeed. The pleasure in this work derives from the ability to match one entry with another, and to retain a transparent texture throughout.

Octet no. 8
Canzon XXVIII (1608)
Choir 1: Tr I II Hn (Tb/Tr) Tb
Choir 2: Tr I II Hn (Tb/Tr) Tb

This popular canzona in the conventional quartet style requires a pair of fairly confident trumpeters. The opening is very exposed, requiring top G's and A's in the very first bars: it would be wise, therefore, not to place this piece right at the start of a programme, but to allow the performers to 'play themselves in' on some other music before. Moreover, most of the rest of the canzona lies fairly high for the first trumpets, and although there is the usual generous supply of breathing spaces, the work as a whole does demand players with a good lip for the high notes. (The work could easily be tranposed down, but some of its brilliance would inevitably be lost.)

Once again, it is important that the longer notes should be given their full value, especially at the ends of phrases, so that the joints in the music should appear absolutely smooth. Failure to observe this procedure always results in very scrappy performances, and a general feeling of insecurity. The A—B—A—B—A structure presents few problems of inter-pretation, and the players should be encouraged to keep something in reserve for the final section, with its repeat of the opening material.

Octet no. 9
Canzon VIII (1615)
Choir 1: Tr I II III(Hn) Tb
Choir 2: Tb I (Hn) II III IV* (Tba)
(*B♭/F)

This canzona, like the *Sonata Pian' e Forte* (Octet no. 6) is written for double quartet with differing instrumental com-binations. As in the *Sonata*, the third part of the first choir generally lies on the low side, and would certainly suit a horn, while the second choir has no trumpet parts and can be played either entirely by trombones, or by horns, trombones, and tuba. It therefore makes an obvious pair, for concert purposes, with the *Sonata*. There are, however, six bars in the middle of

the canzona of somewhat taxing material for the first and
second trumpets, of a level of difficulty which does not occur
in the *Sonata*. For this reason at least, it would be wise to set a
fairly steady tempo. It would be a great pity to pass this work
by simply on account of these six bars, and rather than not
playing it at all, one would urge a slight trimming of the
baroque ornamentation in this section for the sake of the
splendours in the rest of the work. In many respects this is one
of the most fascinating pieces in the whole set of Gabrieli
Canzonas, with its ritornello-like phrases (bars 5, 10, 24, 40,
etc.), its wealth of melodic and rhythmic ideas, and its unusual
textures (44—50 and 72). In order to grasp the work as a
whole the players will have to bring a very disciplined
approach to their performance: the slightest casualness in
matters of note values and phrasing will lead inevitably to a
very incoherent sound.

(See also Octet No. 12.)

Octet no. 10
Canzon X (1615)
Choir 1: Tr I II Tb I (Hn) II
Choir 2: Tr I II Tb I (Hn) II

It would be very unwise to try to hurry this music: the pace
must be determined by the ease with which bars 52—60, for
example, can be accomplished. These splendid sequential
cascades must be allowed to make their full sonorous effect,
and this means that a very broad approach to the opening
phrases is absolutely essential. It will help to count eight to the
bar, and to concentrate on a very legato style in the opening
eight bars: once the semiquavers are reached, the music moves

along quite naturally, and at the arrival of the first of the demisemiquaver clusters at bar 19 comes a further enrichment of the texture. At first these demisemiquaver passages are for solo instruments, but when the idea is taken by two, then three, then four instruments at once, the ensemble discipline has to be very carefully fostered, for raggedness at moments like this can destroy the beauty of the total structure. This is a work that has, perhaps, more in common with Bach and the later Baroque than with the madrigal-like techniques of many of the other canzonas.

The short section from half-way through bar 18 to half-way through bar 22 might be as good a starting point for rehearsal as any: it allows everyone to get used to the balance and the pace immediately. There are many beautiful moments in this canzona, and it easily repays the time spent in preparing a performance.

Octet no. 11
Canzon XI (1615)
Choir 1: Tr I II Tb I (Hn) II (Bar/Euph)
Choir 2: Tr I II Tb I (Hn) II (Bar/Euph)

This work is in complete contrast to No. 10, and a comparison of the two works will show how varied was Gabrieli's approach to various elements in the baroque/late renaissance style. The several pedal points in the bass tend to slow down the momentum of the music, and it is important, therefore, to set quite a quick-moving tempo for this relatively simple, dance-like canzona. The whole approach to the performance of the work must be very light-hearted, and any leaning towards the ponderous is quite inappropriate here. It would be a mistake to hold back the momentum of the triple-time music for fear of not being able to cope with the final three bars of extravagant flourish: much better to simplify the last cadence than miss the point of the rest of the music. A fairly generous *ritardando* might provide a solution.

As is the case with all the antiphonal canzonas, the groups of instruments should be separated in such a way that the echoing and answering of ideas from one group to another is given some special significance. Much of the point of this style of work will be lost on both players and listeners unless a clear space is made between the groups. The inexperienced player tends to spend too much time counting his bars of rests, and not enough time listening to the phrasing of passages that he will himself in due course be imitating. The 'waiting' time in this canzona is rather greater than in some of the other works, but at the same time the ensemble problems are relatively slight.

Octet no. 12
Canzon XII (1615)
Choir 1: Tr I Tb I (Hn) II III
Choir 2: Tr I Tb I (Hn) II III

This work can be performed by the same combination of players that is required for Octets Nos. 6 and 9. This work, however, is for two equal choirs, and is more similar in style to works in the 1597 collection than in the 1615 set. It is concerned with the conventional balance of contrapuntal and block harmony textures, with interchanging four- and three-beat sections. The trumpet parts lie mostly in the middle register and make no great demands upon the players. The alto parts lie rather high for most young trombonists and will probably suit horn players better.

For rehearsal purposes, the correct tempo and phrasing can best be absorbed from first playing through the section bars 17—28 a number of times. Once this part of the work can be played comfortably and coherently, the rest of the canzona should fall into place. Bars 37—40 may need some special attention.

Octet no. 13
Canzon XIII (1615)
Choir 1: Tr I II Tb I (Hn) II
Choir 2: Tr I II Tb I (Hn) II

This is a relatively short work which employs the same techniques of dynamic contrast encountered in the *Sonata Pian' e Forte* (Octet no. 6), but with a much greater use of the higher-pitched instruments. After two bars of $\frac{4}{4}$, in which only three instruments have had time to enter with a rising sequential phrase, the music moves into $\frac{6}{4}$ and a simple chordal texture, never to return to the counterpoint, and only in the last 14 bars to the $\frac{4}{4}$. In comparison with some of the other canzonas in this style, it is almost as if sections containing the further development of the $\frac{4}{4}$ contrapuntal ideas had somehow been mislaid by the original publisher.

For players who want a fairly simple piece of music with plenty of volume contrasts, this canzona will provide a great deal of enjoyment. The piece ends with a highly decorated coda, which like other examples among the 1615 set, can be simplified to suit the individual abilities of players or, with the help of a generous *ritardando*, played at a more leisurely pace.

TEN-PART CANZONAS

There are seven 10-part canzonas, with a second version of the fifth one (which includes parts for organ continuo). Somewhat surprisingly, only three of these are for the double quintet arrangement: the other four are for ten polyphonic parts, extending the multi-voiced techniques that are encountered in Octet No. 7.

All seven canzonas can be played by a standard group of instruments: 4 trumpets or cornets, 2 horns in F or E flat, and 4 trombones (or trombone, baritone, euphonium, tuba), although they may also be played by trumpets and trombones only, demanding up to seven trumpets in No. 1, and six trombones in No. 7. The seven works provide a wide range of interest for a ten-part group. Some of these are relatively straightforward works which can be put together quite easily; others demand quite high standards of ensemble playing. All of them are very rewarding to play.

It must be remembered that ten-part counterpoint calls for a great deal of interdependent playing. Very rarely do players in large orchestras and bands find themselves responsible for holding their melodic line on more or less equal terms with nine other lines as they do in these works. A certain degree of restraint is therefore called for at all times. The occasions for a real fortissimo are rare, but there is a constant demand for well rounded phrases, sprightly rhythms, and a good, clean, non-vibrato tone.

Ten-part Canzona no. 1
Canzon Primi Toni a 10 (1597)
Tr I II III IV
Hn I (Tr V) II (Tr VI)
Tb I (Hn III/Tr VII) II III IV (Tba)

All ten parts have made an entry into the opening contrapuntal exposition by bar 13, and the texture of the music
remains fairly complex until a grand cadence point at 55. This
opening section has several melodic ideas which are passed
from instrument to instrument, and the players need to
attempt an intimate conversational approach to the music,
despite the large numbers involved. The next section, bars
56–74, begins with a very much thinner texture which
demands some legato, quiet playing, and then gradually
rebuilds the ten-part texture. The music of the third section in
triple time calls for some careful balancing of parts, as it is in a
quasi-antiphonal style. The final coda (from bar 99) allows a
fairly broad approach, and it is at this point, and not before,
that more powerful playing becomes appropriate. The B flat
transpositions for trumpets do not rise above high B natural.

Ten-part Canzona no. 2
Canzon Duodecimi Toni a 10 (No. 1) (1597)
Tr I II III IV
Hn I (Tr V) II (Tr VI)
Tb I (Hn) II (Hn) III IV (Tba)

This work differs from No. 1 in only one major respect: it
does not contain the usual triple-time section. In all other
respects – thematic material, tempo, and texture – it is very
closely related indeed. The first motif is fully presented by bar
21, at which point the attention turns to a new phrase starting
with three repeated crotchets. The third motif enters at bar 38
and is subsequently joined by the second idea to produce some
exciting double counterpoint. The first idea returns at 68, and
leads to a characteristic section of rising fourths answered by

sequential falling fifths (89—97). The fourth idea, a rising scale passage, leads to a grand coda in which the second motif again appears. If the players can be helped to understand this structure, and to treat each motif with individual phrasing, then all the elements of this beautifully constructed canzona will fall into place. Some conductors may wish to emphasize the structural elements by appropriate variations in the dynamics of the phrasing. The B flat transpositions for trumpets do not rise above high B natural.

Ten-part Canzona no. 3
Canzon Duodecimi Toni a 10 (No. 2) (1597)
Tr I II III IV
Hn I (Tr V) II (Tr VI)
Tb I (Hn) II (Hn) III IV (Tba)

This is not only the longest of the ten-part canzonas, but also probably the most difficult to perform, demanding first and second trumpeters of considerable skill. However, if the ensemble possess two such players capable of sustained high passage work and double-octave semiquaver scales, then this is a most exciting work to perform. The style is quite different from the first two works in this set, for the renaissance polyphony has been replaced by a baroque concertante style, in which the top two parts play almost continuously throughout the piece, and the remaining eight parts play a mainly supporting role. (It is regrettable that the only British performing edition available at present has chosen to transpose the already high trumpet parts *up a tone*, instead of taking the logical course of providing trombone parts transposed down a tone. No doubt many groups will make their own transpositions.)

Ten-part Canzona no. 4
Canzon Duodecimi Toni a 10 (No. 3) (1597)
Choir 1: Tr I II III IV (Hn) Tb
Choir 2: Hn I (Tr/Tb) II (Tb) Tb I II III (Tba)

This is the first of the double-choir canzonas in the ten-part set. This work is very much in the style of the antiphonal octets, and those groups which enjoy playing the many canzonas in that category will enjoy playing this relatively simple work with the support of two additional players. It must be pointed out, however, that there is rather a lot of waiting about, especially for the second choir, who are not playing for a third of the time, and this may not suit players who like to be involved for most of the duration of a work. When the second choir does enter at bar 30 it is given not the principal motif to develop, but a simple harmonic texture which calls for some neat chording on the part of the trombones. There are some delightful features in the section which leads up to the triple-time episode, and some more concentrated ten-part activity in the concluding section.

There are some written top Bs for transposed trumpet parts.

Ten-part Canzona no. 5
Canzon Duodecimi Toni a 10 (No. 4) (1597)
Choir 1: Tr I II Hn (Tr III) Tb I (Hn) II
Choir 2: Tr I II Hn (Tr III) Tb I (Hn) II

There are two versions of this canzona: the main one for double brass choir, and an alternative one for places which happen to have a couple of organs available for performing realizations of the *basso continuo* parts that Gabrieli provided for Venetian performances.

This is a very grand work with some stunning antiphonal effects. There are one or two short ornate passages for the two first trumpets, but generally the demands made upon the players are not very great, for Gabrieli achieves a splendid sound with relatively simple means. The short echoing phrases will lose all their point if the two groups are not properly spaced apart, as they would have been in their original Venetian setting. The opening tempo must take into consideration the pace at which the few batches of semiquavers can be played, but it must be borne in mind that these occasional baroque flourishes make little sense if they sound at all laborious: better to simplify them than to let them slow the whole work down to a crawl. The players must be encouraged to leave plenty of energy in hand for the last twenty or so bars.

Both first trumpet parts lie in the top register with plenty of high Gs, As, and Bs: two E flat cornets might be useful here, though it is perfectly playable by B flat trumpeters with good lips.

Ten-part Canzona no. 6
Canzon XIV (1615)
Choir 1: Tr I II Hn (Tr III) Tb I II (Tba)
Choir 2: Tr I II Hn (Tr III) Tb I II (Tba)

Although this work is laid out in double quintet style, and does indeed exploit antiphonal techniques to great effect, it also (from bar 56 onwards) introduces some interesting, rich harmonic textures, with the bass line supported by instruments from both choirs. The opening imitative exposition of the first choir is not taken up by the second, which begins immediately with a $\frac{3}{4}$ / $\frac{6}{8}$ episode shared by both choirs. A rhythmically modified version of the initial idea then heralds in a great variety of melodic material which provides the players with a wealth of phrasing details to attend to for ensemble purposes. Those performances which can bring out the rhythmic flexibility of this music are likely to meet with greatest success. There is a high C in one of the trumpet parts, and the trombones (transposed to B flat) have some low E flats to play, so B♭/F instruments will be needed.

Ten-part Canzona no. 7
Canzon XV (1615)
Tr I II III IV Hn I (Tb/Tr) II (Tb/Tr) Tb I (Hn) II (Hn) III IV (Tba)

The last of the ten-part canzonas is based on a rising sequential motif which entirely dominates the whole piece. Apart from some very short episodes and a brief triple-time section (of beguiling simplicity), the whole work is based on the contrapuntal exploitation of the opening phrase. Agreement must be sought right away on the articulation of this phrase, for it is not possible to have differences of opinion on so crucial a matter. Obviously, precise, well-pointed articulation will sound best.

As the main idea is so much in evidence, particular attention must be given to such other material as is present, e.g.

and

There are one or two high Cs in the first trumpet part and a phrase which briefly touches high D. Horns in F have one or two high Gs, while the lowest trombone needs a Bb/F instrument for some low Ebs.

TWELVE-PART CANZONAS

There are five works in this set: four of them are written for the triple-quartet grouping, while the remaining one (*Sonata Octavi Toni*) is written for double six-part choir. The triple-choir works can all be performed by quartets with the following instruments: 2 trumpets or cornets, and 2 trombones (or one trombone and baritone or euphonium) — that is, six trumpets (or cornets) and six trombones (etc.) for each work. There are, however, many other instrumentations possible. Nos. 1, 2, and 4 can comfortably replace the first trombones with horns (F or Eb), thus producing the following quartets: 2 trumpets or cornets, 1 horn (F or Eb), and 1 trombone (or baritone or euphonium).

This is not, however, possible in the case of no. 5, where the parts are too low for horns. It would also be technically possible to substitute french horns for the second trumpet parts in numbers 1, 2, and 4, provided that players who were happy with the top notes were available. Thus a combination of either Tr/Hn/Hn/Tb or Tr/Hn/Tb/Tb is not inconceivable.

The second trumpet part of No. 5 is too high for a horn substitution.

No. 3 in the set (*Sonata Octavi Toni*), like the other Gabrieli sonatas, makes more use of the lower-pitched instruments than of the trumpets, and thus requires a double set of the following instruments: trumpet or cornet and 5 trombones (or 5 from trombones, baritones, euphoniums, tuba); or trumpet or cornet, horn (F or E♭), and 4 trombones (or 4 from trombones, baritones, euphoniums, tuba); or 2 trumpets or cornets (with second part mostly on the low side), horn (F or E♭), and 3 trombones (or 3 from trombones, baritones, euphoniums, tuba).

The problems likely to be encountered in the spacing of the players for the double-choir arrangement have already been discussed. For triple-choir pieces it is again essential that the three groups are properly separated, so that the identity of each group can be clearly established. Finding room for the performance of this type of music is not always easy, for every player must, of course, be able to see the conductor and at the same time feel himself intimately involved in his own quartet.

Such pieces as these are not for everyday use; but they are invaluable for schools with several quartets, as they provide a marvellous opportunity for playing together in a chamber-music context. They are also very suitable for festivals, when two or three schools can join together for a gala performance. Needless to say, they could also be played with an organ replacing one of the groups in an emergency.

Twelve-part Canzona no. 1
Canzon Septimi et Octavi Toni a 12 (1597)
Choirs 1 and 2: Tr I II (Hn) Tb I (Hn) II
Choir 3: The same (except that a tuba could replace Tb II)

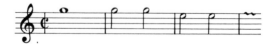

This is a work that will present few problems to players who have already had some experience in quartet playing, for the individual parts are relatively simple, and the magnificent sonorous effects are created without complexity. The canzona begins with all three groups playing a mainly chordal passage. At bar 10 the music breaks down into the three groups, and the broad harmonic textures are freely exchanged betweeen groups. It is absolutely essential that agreement is reached on matters of phrasing and dynamics, and it is particularly important that the groups do not try to out-play each other, especially in the production of volume. As quavers are the quickest notes in this piece, the *alla breve* minim beats must keep the music moving along all the time, and a madrigal-like texture should always be kept in mind. The short triple-time episode must be approached and quitted with as much ease as possible, so that the music does not become sectionalized. In the concluding section it would be a mistake to start a *ritardando* too soon, but the final group of entries can certainly justify a slight broadening out.

Twelve-part Canzona no. 2
Canzon Noni Toni a 12 (1597)
Choirs 1, 2, and 3: Tr I II (Hn) Tb I (Hn) II

In many respects this is in the same mould as No. 1, with similar simple chord progressions passed from group to group, and with no substantial difficulties for any of the individual parts. It is a longer work, however, and there are more periods of inactivity for each group, as each group is given rather longer stretches of the music to play by itself. There is no triple-time section. There are some high Bs in the transposed trumpet parts.

Twelve-part Canzona no. 3
Sonata Octavi Toni a 12 (1597)
Choirs 1 and 2: Tr Tb I (Hn/Tr) II (Hn) III IV V (Tba)

This is the only one of the 12-part canzonas written for double choir, and consequently it is more related to the double-choir 10-part canzonas than to the other 12-part works. As in the other works bearing the title *Sonata*, Gabrieli seems interested in exploiting the colours of the lower brass. The Trombone V parts in both choirs are pretty low throughout the work, and must be played on a B♭/F trombone, or a four-valve euphonium, or better still, an F or E♭ tuba. With six, and sometimes eight, instruments all sustaining melodic lines below middle C, there is a great need for restraint, clear intonation, pointed rhythms, and immaculate phrasing, if the work is not to degenerate into a mournful groan. Make sure that the many rests in the parts are allowed to bring some daylight to the texture. If tubas are used they must play their parts like cellos, not double basses. There are many characteristic antiphonal passages, and a really splendid concluding section.

Twelve-part Canzona no. 4
Canzon XVI (1615)
Choirs 1, 2, and 3: Tr I II (Hn) Tb I (Hn) II

This canzona is rhythmically more exciting than the two 1597 triple-choir works. The playing mostly demands a very light touch and clear articulation. While the individual parts are by no means difficult, the work does call for a strong sense of rhythm based on seventeenth-century principles, and not the more regular phrasing of the eighteenth.

The second and third choirs are kept waiting for their entries; the second goes straight into compound time with its own material, while the third plays a sort of variation on the opening. When the three choirs do join together at bar 30 there is some sizzling counterpoint. This is one of Gabrieli's most rewarding works.

Twelve-part Canzona no. 5
Canzon XVII (1615)
Choirs 1, 2, and 3: Tr I II Tb I II
(There is no real 'middle' texture in this work, and thus no place for horns.)

The arpeggio subject is so unlike the material of any of the other canzonas that this work has a unique flavour about it. The three choirs join together for short ritornello-like statements, while each of the groups develops its own material. Really light, rhythmically alert playing is essential here, with the various rhythmic patterns treated with plenty of sparkle. On B♭ trumpets there are plenty of phrases rising to high B natural, so players confident in the top part of the compass are essential.

There is often a gap of an octave or more between the middle parts in all three choirs, and this unusual texture may at first seem strange to the players. However, they cannot fail to be impressed by this splendid work, which will provide hours of satisfaction.

14, 15, AND 22-PART CANZONAS

The four canzonas in this group provide further music for triple-choir settings, and one work for five choirs. One is drawn from the 1597 pieces (*Canzon Quarti Toni*) and presents no more difficulties in performance than do the two triple-quartet settings in the 1597 group. The other three pieces belong to the 1615 publication and, at least in the trumpet parts, demand a fairly advanced technique on the part of the players. Canzonas XVIII and XIX (1615) in particular do contain extremely florid top parts, and it must be remembered that they were originally written for the *cornetto*. They are, however, by no means impossible for modern trumpets, provided that the overall tempo of the music is not too fast, and that the players develop the right approach to what are, after all, only decorative whirls. A passage such as the following (from Canzon XIX) may at first seem rather off-putting:

but when it is thought of in terms of the following:

with optional passing notes added, the problems seem far less substantial.

These are all works for special occasions, and many young players will be excited by the challenges which they pose. The parts for the lower-pitched instruments are quite straightforward, and if there are two or three skilful trumpeters on hand, these works will certainly provide them with something of interest.

Fourteen-part Canzona
Canzon XVIII (1615)
Choirs 1 and 2: Tr I II Hn (Tb) Tb I II (Bar/Euph)
Choir 3: Hn (Tb) Tb I II (Bar/Euph) III* (Tba)
(*low notes demand a B♭/F trombone, or four-valve euphonium, or tuba)

This canzona has a number of interesting features. The third choir is only of quartet proportions and does not have parts for trumpets. The two quintets, on the other hand, need four trumpeters with a great deal of confidence, for a good deal of fairly elaborate decoration is required from them. The top part of the third choir is also fairly demanding for a horn or trombone player. The structure of the work is itself intriguing: the opening phrase turns up as the bass to countersubjects when both the second and third choirs enter, and is referred to throughout the piece.

Fifteen-part Canzona no. 1
Canzon Quarti Toni a 15 (1597)
Choir 1: Tr I II (Hn/Tb) Hn (Tb) Tb I (Bar/Euph) II* (Tba)
Choir 2: Tr (Hn/Tb) Hn (Tb) Tb I II (Bar/Euph) III* (Tba)
Choir 3: Tr I II (Hn/Tb) Hn (Tb) Tb I (Bar/Euph) II* (Tba)
(*low notes demand a B♭/F trombone, or four-valve euphonium, or tuba)

This is a relatively easy work, similar in style to the triple quartets of the 1597 collection. The choirs are not quite equal in the demands on compass, since the middle group is generally lower. The bass parts of each group demand plenty of bottom Cs, so tubas can find a place in this work provided that they think in cello and not in double bass terms. There is a certain amount of waiting about for each group in the early stages, but there are splendid things worth waiting for.

Fifteen-part Canzona no. 2
Canzon XIX (1615)
Choirs 1, 2, and 3: Tr Hn (Tr/Tb) Tb I (Hn) II (Bar/Euph) III*
(Tba)
(*low notes demand a B♭/F trombone, or four-valve
euphonium, or tuba)

This work is like the 14-part *Canzon XVIII* in the high
demands it makes upon the three top trumpeters, and all that
has already been said about these parts applies here. There is a
lot more to this work, however, than just baroque decoration,
and all the players will find themselves involved in some most
exciting contrapuntal and harmonic effects. Placed at three
points in a fairly resonant building, and with no attempt to
rush the music, players can really enjoy the splendours of this
remarkable Venetian sound.

Twenty-two-part Canzona
Sonata XX (1615)
Choir 1: Tr I II (Hn/Tb) Hn (Tb) Tb I (Hn) II (Bar/Euph) III
(Bar/Euph/Tba)
Choir 2: Tr I II (Hn/Tb) Hn (Tb) Tb (Bar/Euph/Tba)
Choir 3: Hn I (Tb) II (Tb) Tb I (Bar/Euph) II* (Tba)
Choir 4: Tr I II Hn (Tb) Tb (Bar/Euph)
Choir 5: Tr Hn (Tb/Tr) Tb I (Hn Bar/Euph) II (Bar/Euph)
(*low notes demand a B♭/F trombone, or four-valve
euphonium, or tuba)

As the above information suggests, there are many possible
combinations of instruments that can tackle this work,
although five trumpets and seventeen trombones are often
specified. In order to use a school's resources to maximum
effect the following figures may prove useful:

	Minimum	Maximum
Trumpets/cornets	5	8
Horns	0	10
Trombones	3	17
Bar/Euph	0	7
Tubas	0	3

It is clear that most brass bands have the resources to cover these requirements, provided that they have a horn and a trombone extra to minimum contest requirements. However, the obvious occasion for the performance of this work is at festivals, where five schools can get together for a special performance. It has to be admitted that the fifth group does have to wait some time before making its entry, but what magnificent material it has to present! With such large numbers involved the need for clear articulation, light dynamics, precise rhythms, and exact note values becomes all the greater. There is also a major problem in seating the players. The five groups must be spaced apart, but any one group must not be so far from another that it cannot hear what is going on. If these difficulties can be overcome, then many people will get a great deal of pleasure out of the performance of this fascinating work.

The canzonas of Giovanni Gabrieli represent only a small part of the output of his period. Players who enjoy playing Gabrieli should also investigate works by the following composers:

Adson, J. *d.c.* 1640
Antegnati, C. 1557–*c.* 1620
Banchieri, A. 1567–1634
Brade, W. *c.* 1560–1630
Byrd, W. 1538–1623
Chilese, B. *fl. c.* 1600

Franck, M. *c.* 1579—1639
Frescobaldi, G. 1583—1643
Gabrieli, A. *c.* 1520—86
Grillo, G. B. *d.c.* 1622
Guami, G. *c.* 1540—1611
Holborne, A. *d.* 1602
Lappi, P. *fl. c.* 1615
Luzzaschi, L. 1545—1607
Maschera, F. *c.* 1535—84
Massaino, T. *c.* 1550—*c.* 1609
Merulo, C. 1533—1604
Monteverdi, C. 1567—1643
Praetorius, M. 1571—1621
Scheidt, S. 1587—1654
Schein, J. H. 1586—1630
Schutz, H. 1585—1672
Sweelinck, J. P. 1562—1621
Tomkins, T. 1572—1656

From the latter part of the seventeenth century, brass transcriptions of works by the following composers are also of lasting interest:

Buxtehude, D. *c.* 1637—1707
Coleman, C. *fl. c.* 1650
Locke, M. *c.* 1630—1677
Pezel, J. C. 1639—94
Purcell, H. 1659—95
Reiche, G. 1667—1734
Rosenmüller, J. *c.* 1619—84

For details of works by these and other composers, reference should be made to the catalogues that follow.

The Music

A list of available published material for brass instruments with piano and for brass ensembles

The following is a list of compositions currently available in the British Isles.* It includes both works published in the British Isles and those that are available through importers. Only the name of the British importing agent is listed for foreign publications in order to simplify purchasing problems. The one exception to this is the Robert King Co., whose publications are available from a number of sources, including June Emerson, Ampleforth, York; W. & G. Foyle Ltd., London; Boosey & Hawkes Ltd., London; and Blackwell's Music Shop, Oxford.

List of publishers:

B & C   British and Continental Music Agencies Ltd., 8 Horse and Dolphin Yard, London W1V 7LG.

BH   Boosey & Hawkes Ltd., 295 Regent Street, London W.1.

B   Bärenreiter Edition, 32 Great Titchfield Street, London W.1.

BR   Breitkopf & Härtel Ltd. (see B & C)

C   Chappell & Co. Ltd., 50 New Bond Street, London W.1.

*Publishers' catalogues form the principal source of this list. For information on material no longer available for purchase, readers are advised to consult lists in books by Gregory, Rasmussen, Wick, and others (see bibliography).

C	J. & W. Chester Ltd., 7 Eagle Court, London E.C.1.
E	June Emerson, Ampleforth, York.
F	Faber Music Ltd., 38 Russell Square, London W.C.1.
H	Hinrichsen/Peters Edition Ltd., 10–12 Baches Street, London N.1.
K	Robert King Music Co., N. Easton, Mass., U.S.A. (*see* Emerson).
KP	Keith Prowse Music Publishing Co. Ltd., 21 Denmark Street, London W.C.2.
L	Alfred Lengnick & Co. Ltd., 241a Brighton Road, S. Croydon, Surrey.
MR	Musica Rara, 2 Great Marlborough Street, London W.1.
N	Novello & Co. Ltd., Borough Green, Sevenoaks, Kent.
NWM	New Wind Music Co., 23 Ivor Place, London N.W.1.
OUP	Oxford University Press, 44 Conduit Street, London W1R 0DE.
R	G. Ricordi Ltd., The Bury, Church Street, Chesham, Bucks.
Sch	G. Schirmer, 140 Strand, London WC2R 1HH.
S	B. Schott & Son Ltd., 48 Great Marlborough Street, London W.1.
SB	Stainer & Bell Ltd. & Galliard Ltd., Queen Anne's Road, Great Yarmouth, Norfolk.
Univ	Universal Edition, 2–3 Fareham Street, London W.1.
UMP	United Music Publishers Ltd., 1 Montague Street, London W.C.1.
W	J. Weinberger, 10–16 Rathbone Street, London W.1.

Instrumentation: The following abbreviations are used:

Tr = trumpet in B♭ (other keys specified)
Ct = cornet
Tb = trombone
Hn = horn in F (other keys specified)
Tba = tuba

Bar = baritone horn
Euph = euphonium
Pf = pianoforte
Perc = percussion
Brackets indicate alternative instruments, e.g.: Tr I II (Hn) Hn
(Tb) Tb Tba = first B♭ trumpet, second B♭ trumpet or horn in
F, horn in F or trombone, trombone, and tuba.

The smaller publishers in the U.S.A.
Many smaller firms in America are very interested in brass
publications, but copies of their works are not always easy to
obtain in this country. For players who have exhausted the
material provided in the following lists, application could be
made to such companies as Abingdon, Ann Arbor, Boston
Music, Colombo, Concordia, Marks, Modern Brass Ensemble,
and Western International.

	Composer	*Title*	*Instruments*	*Publisher*
1	Abbot, A.	Alla Caccia	Hn Pf	Univ
2	Abbott, G. J.	Trumpeters Three	Tr I II III	Univ
3	Adler, S.	Sonata	Hn Pf	K
4		Five movements	Tr I II Hn Tb Tba	K
5		Praeludium	Tr I II Hn I II Tb I II III (Bar) Tba (optional Perc)	K
6		Concert Piece	Tr I II III Hn I II III Tb I II III IV (Bar) V (Bar) Tba Perc	K
7		Divertimento	As above	K
8		Five Vignettes	Tb I-XII	OUP
9	Addison, J.	Concerto for Trumpet	Tr Pf	SB
10		Divertimento	Tr I II Hn Tb	SB
11	Adson, J.	Two airs for cornetts and sackbuts	Tr I II Tb I(Hn) II III(Bar)	K

	Composer	Title	Instruments	Publisher
12		Three courtly masquing ayres (1621)	Tr I II Tb I II III	S
13	Ahlgrimm, H.	Concerto in F (1938)	Tr Pf	H
14	Albinoni, T.	Concerto in F	Tr Pf	UMP
15		Concerto in D minor	Tr Pf	UMP
16		Adagio in G minor	Tr Pf	R
17	Alexander, J.	Sonata	Tb Pf	N
18	Alford, K. J.	Colonel Bogey	Tr I II Hn Tb	BH
19	Altenburg, J. E.	Concerto (1795)	Tr I II III IV V VI VII Perc	K
20		Fugue and Polonaise	Tr I II (III)	H
21	Altenburg, J. E. and others	Old Wind Music (includes Franck, Scheidt, & Reiche)	Ensemble (4- & 5-part)	H
22	Alwyn, W.	Fanfare for a Joyful Occasion	Tr I II III Hn I II III IV Tb I II III Tba Perc	OUP
23	Ameller, A.	Hauterine	Tba (Tb) Pf	UMP
24		Rivière du Loup	Tb Pf	UMP
25		Trois-Rivières	Tr Pf	UMP
26		Three Easy Pieces	Hn Pf	H
27		Chorale	Tb I II III IV	H
28	Amram, D.	Fanfare & Processional	Tr I II Hn Tb Tba	H
29	Andersen, E.	Sonatina	Tb Pf	C
30	Anon.	Bläser-Intraden	Ensemble (4-part)	B
31		24 Early German Chorales	Tb I II III IV	K
32	Angerer, P.	Quartet	Hn I II III IV	Univ
33	Antegnati, C.	Canzona 9	Tr I II Tb I (Hn) II	MR
34		Canzona 20	Tr I II Tb I (Hn) II III	MR
35	Arnell, R.	Music for Horns	Hn I II III IV	E
36		Trumpet Allegro Op. 58 No. 2	Tr Pf	S
37	Arnold, J. (arr.)	Early Trumpet Solos	Tr Pf or Tb Pf	BH
38		Early Trumpet Solos and Duets	{ Tr Pf or Tb Pf { Tr I II Pf	BH
39	Arnold, M.	Quintet (1961)	Tr I II Hn Tb Tba	P

	Composer	Title	Instruments	Publisher
40		Horn Concerto (2nd Mvt)	Hn Pf	L
41		Fantasy for Trumpet	Tr	F
42		Fantasy for Horn	Hn	F
43		Fantasy for Trombone	Tb	F
44		Fantasy for Tuba	Tba	F
45	Atterberg, K.	Concerto Op. 28	Hn Pf	B
46	Auclert, P.	Lied	Hn Pf	UMP
47	Bach, C. P. E.	Sonata in G minor	Tr Pf	UMP
48		March (Fanfare)	Tr I II III (optional Perc)	BH
49	Bach, J. S. (arr. Lake)	Sixteen Chorales	Any quartet	Sch
50	Bach, J. S.	Cantata 118	Tr I II III IV Hn I II Tb I II III IV	K
51		Bist du bei mir	Tr (Tb) Pf	R
52		Rondeau et badinerie	Tr Pf	UMP
53		Aria	Hn Pf	UMP
54		Prelude and Fugue	Tr I II Tb I II	BH
55		Four Chorales	Ensemble	Univ
56		Organ Prelude & Fugue	Tr I II Hn Tb	Univ
57		Finale from *St. John Passion*	Tr I II III Tb I II III Tba	UMP
58		Fugues in four parts	Tr I II Hn Tb	Univ
59		Four Chorales	Ensemble (4-part)	Univ
60		A Bach Suite	Ensemble (4-part)	OUP
61		Jesu, nun sei gepreiset	Tr I II III Pf (Organ)	K
62		Nun danket alle Gott	Tr I II III Pf (Organ)	K
63		16 Chorales	Tb I II III IV	K
64		Alleluia (Cantata 142)	Tr I II Tb I II Organ	K
65		In dulci Jubilo	Tr I II Tb (Hn) II Organ	K
66		Jesu, nun sei gepreiset	As above	K
67		*Art of Fugue* I, III, & IV	Tr I II Hn Tb I II (Bar)	K

	Composer	Title	Instruments	Publisher
68		Ricercar from *Musical Offering*	Tr I II III Hn (Tb) Tb I II III (Bar)	K
69		Fugue no. 14 from *Art of Fugue*	Tr I II Tb I II Tba	SB
70		Sarbande & Bourrée	Ensemble (4-part)	BH
71		Vor himmel hoch	Ensemble (4-part)	BH
72	(ed. Johnson)	Chorales	Tr I II E♭ Hn Tb/Bar	N
73		Chorales	Tr I II III IV	N
74	Bach—Gounod	Ave Maria	Hn (Tr) Pf	H
75	Badings, H.	Three Netherland Dances	Tr I II Hn Tb	L
76	Baines, F.	Pastorale	Tr Pf	S
77		Three short pieces	Tr Tb	SB
78	Baker, E.	Cantilena	Hn Pf	C
79	Baker, M.	Trumpet tango	Tr Pf	E
80		Alla polacca	Tr Pf	E
81	Baldassare, P.	Sonatas 1 & 2	Tr Pf	MR
82	Banchieri, A.	Canzoni alla francese (10, 11)	Tr I II Tb I (Hn) II	MR
83	Bargagni	Canzona 'La Monteverde'	Tr I II Tb I (Hn) II	MR
84	Bark, J. & Rabe, F.	Bolos	Tb I II III IV	C
85		Polonaise	Tb I II III IV	C
86	Barsham, E. (arr.)	Shore's Trumpet	Tr Pf	BH
87		Ten Trumpet Tunes	Tr Pf	OUP
88	Bartók, B. (arr. Stratton, D)	For Children (five pieces)	Tr I II Hn Tb	BH
89	Bartolino, O.	Canzon 30	Tr I II III IV Tb I (Hn) II (Hn) III IV	MR
90	Bassett, L.	Sonata	Hn Pf	K
91		Sonata	Tb Pf	K
92		Quartet	Tb I II III IV	K
93	Bates, W.	Flourishes for Brass	Tr I II or Hn I II	Ch
94	Baudach, U.	Te Deum laudamus	Tr I II III Tb I II III Organ	B
95	Baversdorf, T.	Cathedral Music	Tr I II Tb I II (Bar) Organ or Tr I II III	K

	Composer	Title	Instruments	Publisher
			IV Hn I II III Tb I II III Bar/Tba	
96	Bazelon, I.	Quintet	Tr I II (in C) Hn Tb I II (Tba)	BH
97	Beck, C.	Intermezzo	Hn Pf	UMP
98	Beckerath, A.	Tower Music	Tr I II III Tb I II III	H
99	Beeler (arr.)	29 Cornet Solos	Tr Pf	Sch
100		12 Pieces	Tr Pf	Sch
101	Beethoven, L.	Nature's Adoration	Tr I II Hn (in E♭) Tb (Bar/Euph)	H
102		Cavatina from String Quartet Op. 130	Hn Pf	H
103		Sonata Op. 17	Hn Pf	B/BH/ H/Sch
104		Three Equali	Tb I (Tr) II III IV	B/BH/ K
105	Benger, R.	Preludes & Canons	Tr I II III	C
106		Miniature Suite	Tr I II Pf	C
107	Bentley, A. (arr.)	XVIth-Century Quartets	Any quartet	C
108		XVth-Century Trios	Tr I II Hn (in E♭ or F, or Tb)	Ch
109	Bentzon, N. V.	Sonata Op. 47	Hn Pf	C
110		Sonata Op. 73	Tr Pf	C
111		Trio Op. 82	Hn Tr Tb	C
112	Berger, J.	Intrada	Tr I II Tb I (Hn) II	K
113	Bergmann, W.	Seven Canonic Studies	Tr I II (Hn I II)	S
114	Bertali	Six Short Pieces	Tr I II Tb I II III	MR
115	Beversdorf, T.	Three Epitaphs	Tr I II Hn Tb	BH
116	Biber, H.	Sonata a 7	Tr I II III IV V VI (optional Perc)	Univ
117	Binkerd, G.	Three Canzonas	Tr I II III Hn I II III Tb I II III Tba	BH
118	Blacher, B.	Divertimento Op. 131	Tr Tb Pf	S
119	Bliss, A.	Fanfare for Heroes	Tr I II III Tb I II III Perc	N
121		Fanfare for the Lord Mayor of London	Tr I III III Hn I–IV Tb I II III Tba (optional Perc)	K

	Composer	Title	Instruments	Publisher
122		Royal Fanfares	Tr I II III/Tb I II III Tba Perc	N
123	Bloch, W.	Partita	Tr I II III IV (optional Perc)	Univ
124		Festival Music	Tr I—VII Tb I II III Tba (optional Perc)	Univ
125	Boda, J.	Sonatina	Tb (Tba) Pf	K
126	Bogar, I.	Three Movements	Tr I II Hn Tb	BH
127	Bogar, M.	Three Hungarian Folksongs	Tr I II Hn Tb	BH
128	Bond, C.	Trumpet Concerto	Tr Pf	BH
129	Bonelli, A.	Toccata 'Athalanta'	Tr I II Hn I II Tb I—IV (optional Perc)	K
130	Borroff, E.	Sonata	Hn Pf	K
131	Borst, R. & Bogar, I.	Trumpet Music for Beginners	Tr Pf	BH
132	Botti	Three Pieces	Tr Pf	H
133	Bourguignon	Recitative and Rondo Op. 94	Tr Pf	H
134	Boutry, R.	Five Pieces	Tb I II III IV	UMP
135	Bozza, E.	Cornettina	Ct (Tr) Pf	UMP
136		Badinage	Tr Pf	UMP
137		Three pieces	Tb I II III IV (Tba)	UMP
138		Hommage à Badi	Tb Pf	UMP
139		Suite	Hn I II III IV	UMP
140		En Irlande	Hn Pf	UMP
141	Brade, W.	Dances & Canzonas (1617)	Tr I II Tb I II III	MR
142		Two Pieces	Tr I II Tb I (Hn) Tb II III (Bar)	K
143	Bradford—Anderson, M.	March in Canon	Hn Pf	BH
144	Brahms, J.	Lullaby	Tr Pf	BH
145		Intermezzo Op. 119 No. 3	Hn Pf	OUP
146		Scherzo (Serenade in D)	Hn Pf	OUP
147		Es ist ein Ros' entsprungen	Tr I II (Hn) Hn Tb I II (Bar)	K
148		O Welt, ich muss dich lassen	Tr I II Organ Tb I (Hn) II (Bar)	K

	Composer	Title	Instruments	Publisher
149	Bramieri, C.	Canzona 'La Foccara'	Ensemble — 8-part (2 x 4)	H
150	Brandt, V.	Two Pieces	Tr I II Pf	Univ
151	Britten, B.	Fanfare for St. Edmundsbury	Tr (in C) I II III	BH
152	Brown, C.	Légende	Hn Pf	UMP
153	Bruneau, A.	Romance	Hn Pf	UMP
154	Buchtger, F.	Four Little Pieces	Tb Pf	B
155	Buonamente, G. B.	Sonata	Tr I II Hn I (Tr) Hn II (Tb) Tb I II (Bar) Tba	K
156		Canzon a 5	Tr I II Tb I II III	MR
157	Burgon, G.	Fanfares and Variants	Tr I II Tb I II	SB
158		Trio	Tr I II Tb	SB
159		Lullaby and Aubade	Tr Pf	SB
160		Toccata	Tr Pf	SB
161		Divertimento	Tr I II Hn Tb (or any quartet)	CH
162		Five Studies	Tr I II Tb I II	CH
163	Burkhard, N.	Romance	Hn Pf	B
164	Burnett, M.	Suite Blaen Myherin	Tr I II Tb I II	R
165	Bush, A.	Autumn Poem	Hn Pf	S
166		Trent's Broad Reaches	Hn Pf	S
167	Bush, G.	Homage to Matthew Locke	Tr I II III Tb I II III	SB
168	Busser, H.	Andante et Scherzo	Tr Pf	UMP
169	Butt, J.	Suite	Hn Pf	H
170	Butterworth, A.	Romanza	Hn Pf	H
171		Trio (1962)	Tr Hn Tb	F
172		Three Dialogues	Tr I II	H
173		Scherzo	Tr I II Hn (in E♭) Tb (Bar/Euph)	H
174	Butterworth, N.	Prelude and Scherzo	Hn Pf	CH
175		Tudor Suite	Tr I II Hn Tb (or any quartet)	CH
176		Four motets for brass	As above	CH
177	Cacavas	Serenade in Gold	Tb I II III IV	BH
178	Campra, A.	Rigaudon	Tr I II Tb I (Hn) II	K
179	Capuzzi, A.	Andante and Rondo (Concerto for Double Bass)	Tb (Tba) Pf	H

	Composer	Title	Instruments	Publisher
180	Carse, A.	Two Easy Pieces	Hn Pf	SB
181	Castelnuovo-Tedesco, M.	Chorale and Variation Op. 162	Hn I II III IV	E
182	Catalinet, P.	Divertissements	Hn I II III IV or Tb I II III IV	H
183		Caprice	Hn Pf	H
184		Ten Little Indians	Hn Pf	H
185		Suite in Miniature	Tba I II	H
186	Cavaccio	Two Canzonas	Tr I II Tb I (Hn) II	MR
187	Cazzati, M.	La Cappara	Tr Pf	MR
188		La Zambecari	Tr Pf	MR
189	Cesti, P. A.	Prelude to *Il pomo d'oro*	Tr I II III IV V VI Hn I II III IV Tb I II III IV (Euph)	Univ
190	Chagrin, F.	Divertimento	Tr I II Hn Tb Tba	SB
191		Fanfare for Adam	Tb I II III	N
192	Charpentier, J.	Quatuor de forme liturgique	Tb I II III IV	UMP
193	Chase, A.	Passacaglia for 10 Trombones	Tb I II III IV V VI VII VIII IX X	E
194	Chilese, B.	Canzon 22 (1608)	Tr I II III (Hn) Tb I II	MR
195		Canzoni 31 and 32 (1608)	Tr I II III IV Tb I (Hn) II (Hn) III IV	MR
196	Coker, W.	Concerto	Tb Pf	Univ
197	Cole, H.	The Hammersmith Gallop	Tr Pf	S
198	Coleman, C.	Four Pieces for Sackbuts and Cornetts	Tr I II Tb I II III or Tr I II Hn (in E♭) Tb Euph	OUP
199	Connolly, J.	Cinquepaces Op. 5	Tr I II Hn Tb Tba	OUP
200	Cook, K.	Impromptu	Tr Pf	H
201	Cooke, A.	Rondo in B flat	Hn Pf	S
202	Copland, A.	Fanfare for the Common Man	Tr I II Hn I II III IV Tb I II III Tba Perc	BH
203	Corelli, A.	Adagio and Pastorale	Tr I II Hn Tb	Univ
204		Sonata Op. 5 No. 8	Tr Pf	R
205		Christmas Pastoral	Tr I II Hn I (Tr) II (Tb) Tb I II	K

	Composer	Title	Instruments	Publisher
207	Corrette, M.	Concerto 'La Choisy'	Hn Pf	H
208	Couperin, F.	Fugue	Tr I II Tb I (Hn) II	K
209		Two pieces	As above	K
210		Sarabande and Carillon	As above	K
211		Chaconne	As above (and Organ)	K
212	Cowell, H.	Hymn and Fuguing Tune No. 13	Tb Pf	Sch
213		Rondo	Tr I II III Hn I II Tb I II III	H
214	Cruft, A.	Four English Keyboard Pieces	Tr I II Hn Tb	SB
215		Fanfares	Tr I II III IV V VI (optional Perc)	SB
216		Diversion	Tr I II Hn I II Tb I II	SB
217	Damase, J.-M.	Pavane variée	Hn Pf	UMP
218		Berceuse Op. 19	Hn Pf	UMP
219	Daquin, L. C.	Swiss Carol	Tr I II III Pf (Organ)	K
220	Darcy	Trio	Tr I II III	BH
221	Dart, T. (arr.)	Suite from the Royal Brass Music of King James I	Tr I II III Tb I II III (optional IV)	OUP
222	Dearnley, C. H. (arr.)	8 Easy Pieces by Classical Composers for Solo Brass & Piano	Hn (Tr or Tb) Pf	C
223		More Easy Pieces by Classical Composers for one or two Solo Brass Instruments & Piano	Hn I II (Tr I II or Tb I II) Pf	C
224	Debussy, C.	Fanfare *Le Martyre de Saint-Sebastien*	Tr I II Hn I II III IV V Tb I II III Tba Perc	UMP
225	Defossez, R.	Les Gammes en vacances	Tr Pf	UMP
226	de Haan, S.	Six Short Pieces	Tr I II III Tb I II III	H
227	Dickinson, P.	Fanfares and Elegies	Tr I II III Tb I II III Organ	N

	Composer	Title	Instruments	Publisher
228		Music for Brass (1954)	Tr I II III Tb I II	N
229	Diemer, E. L.	Declamation	Tr I II III IV Hn I II Bar Tb Tba Perc	UMP
230	Domroese, W.	Little Suite	Tb Pf	B
231		Two Epigrams	Tb Pf	B
232		Six Short Pieces	Tr (Hn or Tb) Pf	B
233		Sakura (Japanese Impression)	Tb Pf	UMP
234	Donato, A.	Sonatina	Tr I II III	Sch
235		Prelude and Allegro	Tr Pf	UMP
236	Donizetti (arr.)	Recitative & Cavatina	Hn Pf	H
237	Dorward, D.	Divertimento	Tr I II Hn I II Tb I II Tba	SB
238	Douane, J.	En forêt d'Olonne	Hn Pf	UMP
239	Drakeford, R.	Tower Music	Tr I II Hn Tb Tba (Tb II)	N
240	Dubois, P. M.	Quartet	Tb I II III IV	UMP
241		Quartet	Hn I II III IV	UMP
242	Duck, L.	The Silver Huntress	Hn Pf	H
243		Three Tone Sketches	Tr Pf	H
244	Dufaye, J. M.	Four Pieces (1954)	Tb I II III IV	UMP
245	Dukas, P.	Villanelle	Hn Pf	UMP
246		Fanfare *La Péri*	Tr I II III Hn I II III (optional IV) Tb I II III Tba	UMP
247	Dvořák, A.	Slavonic Dance No. 10	Hn Pf	Ch
248	Eder, H.	Sonatina	Hn Pf	Univ
249	Ehmann, W. and others	Twelve Chorale Partitas	Tr I II (optional III IV) Tb I II (optional III) Perc	B B
250	Ehmann, W. (arr.)	151 Chorale Duets	Tr I II or Tb I II	B
251	Ehmann, W. and others	Neue Spielmusik	Tr I II (optional III) Tb I II (optional III)	B
252		Alte Spielmusik für Bläser: 18 Partitas (Books 1 & 2)	Tr I II (optional III) Hn I (optional II) Tb I II (optional III)	B
253	Enesco, G.	Legend	Tr Pf	Univ

	Composer	*Title*	*Instruments*	*Publisher*
254	Erdmann (arr.)	English Duets	Tr I II	B
255	Fantini, G.	Eight Sonatas	Tr Organ	MR
256		Pieces for Trumpet and Basso Continuo	Tr Pf	B
257	Fiévet, P.	Rondo	Tr Pf	UMP
258	Filippi, A. de	Divertimento	Bar/Euph Tba	K
259	Fiocco, J.	Allegro	Tr Pf	Univ
260	Fitzgerald (arr.)	English Suite	Tr Pf	Univ
261	Flagello, N.	Chorale & Episode for 10 Brass Instruments	Tr I II (in C) Hn I II III IV Tb I II III Tba	N
262		Lyric for Brass Sextet	Tr I II III (in C) Hn Tb I II	N
263		Concertino	Ens Pf Perc	N
264	Forbes, W.	A second Classic & Romantic Album	Tr Pf	OUP
265		A third Classic and Romantic Album	Tr Pf	OUP
266	Frackenpohl, A.	Quartet	Tr I II Tb I (Hn) II	K
267		Quintet	Tr I II Hn Tb Tba	UMP
268		Concertino	Tba Pf	K
269		Sonatina	Tr Pf	Sch
270		Suite	Tr Pf	Sch
271		Trio	Tr Hn Tb	E
272	Francisque, A.	Suite from *Le Trésor d'Orphée*	Tr I II Hn I II Tb I II III (Bar)	UMP
273	Frangkiser, C.	Entry of the Heralds	Tr I II Hn Tb Euph Tba	BH
274	Franck, M.	Intrada (1608)	Tr I II III Tb I II III	B
275		Two Pavans	Tr I II Hn Tb I II (Bar)	B
276	Frehse, A.	Twelve Horn Trios	Hn I II III	BH
277	French Album	Couperin, Lully, etc.	Tr I II Hn Tb	Univ
278	Frescobaldi, G.	Canzon 13	Tr I II Tb I (Hn) II	MR
279		Canzon 21	Tr I II Tb I (Hn) II III	MR
280		Canzon 29	Tr I II III IV Tb I (Hn) II III IV	MR
281		Canzona a 8 in G	Eight-part ensemble	Univ

	Composer	Title	Instruments	Publisher
282		Gagliarda	Tr I II Hn Tb	Sch
283	Fricker, P. R.	Sonata	Hn Pf	S
284	Gabrieli, A.	Ricercare del Sesto Tuono	Tr I II Tb I (Hn) II	MR
285		Ricercare del Duodecimo Tuono	Tr I II Tb I (Hn) II	MR
	Gabrieli, G.	Canzonas from *Sacrae symphoniae* (1597)	(For details see Appendix)	
286		1 Primi toni	a8 (2 × 4)	MR/K
287		2 Septimi toni (i)	a8 (2 × 4)	MR/K/ H
288		3 Septimi toni (ii)	a8 (2 × 4)	MR/K
289		4 Noni toni	a8 (2 × 4)	MR/K
290		5 Duodecemi toni	a8 (2 × 4)	MR
291		6 Sonata pian' e forte	a8 (2 × 4)	MR/ OUP/ K/H
292		7 Primi toni	a10	MR/H
293		8 Duodecimi toni (i)	a10	MR
294		9 Duodecimi toni(ii)	a10	MR
295		10 Duodecimi toni (iii)	a10 (2 × 5)	MR/ K/H
296		11 Duodecimi toni (iv)	a10 (2 × 5)	MR
297		12 Above in 'echo' version		MR
298		13 Septimi toni & Octavi toni	a12 (3 × 4)	MR
299		14 Noni toni	a12 (3 × 4)	MR/H/ E
300		15 Sonata Octavi toni	a12 (2 × 6)	MR/K
301		16 Quarti toni	a15 (3 × 5)	MR/K/ F
		Canzonas from *Canzoni per sonare* (1608)	(See Appendix)	
302		1 (numbers in 1608 edition)	a4	MR/K
303		2	a4	MR/K
304		3	a4	MR/K
305		4	a4	MR

Composer	Title	Instruments	Publisher
306	27	a8	MR
307	28	a8 (2 × 4)	MR
	Canzonas from *Canzoni e sonate* (1615)	(See Appendix)	
308	1	a5	MR/ UMP (Heu-gel)*
309	2	a6	MR/ UMP*
310	3	a6	MR/ UMP*
311	4	a6	MR/ UMP*
312	5	a7	MR/ UMP*
313	6	a7	MR/ UMP*/ H
314	7	a7	MR/ UMP*
315	8	a8 (2 × 4)	MR/ UMP*
316	9	a8	MR/ UMP*
317	10	a8 (2 × 4)	MR/ UMP*
318	11	a8 (2 × 4)	MR/ UMP*
319	12	a8 (2 × 4)	MR/ UMP*
320	13	a8 (2 × 4)	MR/ UMP*/ H
321	14	a10 (2 × 5)	MR/ UMP*
322	15	a10	MR/ UMP*

*Heugel editions (UMP) include parts for strings and woodwind.

	Composer	Title	Instruments	Publisher
323		16	a12 (3 x 4)	MR/ UMP*/ H
324		17	a12 (3 x 4)	MR/ UMP*
325		18	a14 (5 + 5 + 4)	MR/ UMP*
326		19	a15 (3 x 5)	MR/ UMP*
327		20 Sonata	a22 (6 + 4 + 4 + 4 + 4)	MR/ UMP*
328	(arr. Draper)	O magnum mysterium	Tr I II III Hn I II III Tb I II	OUP
329	(arr. Anthony)	Antiphony no. 2	Tr I II Hn I II Tb I II III (Euph) IV (Tba)	Univ
330	Gagnebin, H.	Sarabande	Tb Pf	UMP
331	Galliard, J. E.	Six Sonatas (Bassoon)	Tb Pf	H
332	Gardner, J.	Theme and Variations Op. 7	Tr I II Hn Tb	OUP
333		Romance	Tb Pf	S
334	Gastoldi, G. G.	Spielstücke (1598)	Tr I II	B
335	Gattermeyer, H.	Divertimento	Tr I II Hn I II Tb I II (optional Perc)	Univ
336	Genzmer, H.	Sonatina	Hn Pf	H
337		Sonatina	Tr Pf	H
338		Music for Four Wind Instruments	Tr I II Tb I II	H
339	Gibbons, O. (arr. Cruft)	Suite	Tr Pf	SB
340	Glass, P.	Brass Sextet	Tr I II Hn I II Tb Tba	N
341	Glasser, S.	Trio	Tr I II Tb	MR
342	Glazounov, A.	In modo religioso	Tr I II (Hn) Tb I (Hn) II	K
343	Glinka, M. I.	Four Short Fugues	Tr Tb	K
344	Gow, D.	Suite	Tb I II III IV	MR
345		Serenata	Tr Pf	NWM
346	Gräfe, F.	Concerto in B flat	Tr Pf	L
347	Granados, E.	Spanish Dance No. 5	Hn Pf	OUP

*Heugel editions (UMP) include parts for strings and woodwind.

	Composer	Title	Instruments	Publisher
348	Gregson, E.	Quintet	Tr I II (in C) Hn Tb Tba	N
349		Divertimento	Tb Pf	C
350	Greig (arr. Cook)	Six Popular Melodies	Tr Pf	H
351	Greig, E.	Ballade	Hn Pf	OUP
352		Notturno Op. 54 No. 4	Hn Pf	OUP
353		Funeral March	Tr I II III Hn I II III IV Tb I II III IV (Euph) Tba Perc	K
354		Sarabande (Holberg Suite)	Tb Pf	C
355	Grétry, A.	Serenade	Hn Pf	UMP
356	Grillo, G. B.	Canzon Quarta	Tr I II III IV Tb I (Hn) II (Hn) III IV	MR
357		Canzon 14, 15, 16 (1608)	Tr I II Tb I (Hn) II	MR
358		2 Canzonas a8	Ensemble (2 x 4)	H
359	Gröndahl	Concerto	Tb Pf	C
360	Grossi, A.	Sonata Decima	Tr Pf	MR
361	Guami, G.	Canzona 19	Tr I II Tb I (Hn) II III	MR
362		Canzona 24, 25	Tr I II III IV Tb I (Hn) II (Hn) III IV	MR
363		La Guamina	Tr I II Tb I (Hn) II	MR
364		Canzonas 6, 17	Tr I II Tb I (Hn) II	MR
365	Guilmant, A.	Morceau Symphonique	Tb Pf	S
366	Gussago, C.	'La Porcellaga' a8	Ensemble (2 x 4)	H
367	Hader, W.	Duet	Tr Tb	B
368	Haines, E.	Toccata	Tr I II Tb I (Hn) II	K
369		Sonata for Brass Quintet	Tr I II Hn Tb Tba	K
370	Hamilton, I.	Five Scenes	Tr Pf	Univ
371		Capriccio (1952)	Tr Pf	S
372		Quintet	Tr I II Hn Tb Tba	S
373		Aria	Hn Pf	S
374		Sonata Notturna	Hn Pf	S

	Composer	Title	Instruments	Publisher
375		Capriccio	Tr Pf	S
376	Handel, G. F.	Harmonious Blacksmith	Tr Pf	R
377	(arr. Catelinet)	Sarabande and Bourrée	Tr I II Hn (in E♭) Tb/Bar/Euph	H
378		Adagio and Allegro	Tr Pf	Univ
379		Aria and Bourrée	Tr Pf	Univ
380		A Handel Solo Album	Tr (Tb) Pf	OUP
381		Concertino	Tr Pf	OUP
382		Bourrée and Minuet from Fireworks Music	Tr I II Tb I (Hn) II	K
383		March and Gavotte	Tr I II (Hn) Tb I (Hn) II	K
384		Overture *Berenice*	Tr I II III (Hn) Tb I (Hn) II (Bar)	K
385		Three pieces from *Water Music*	Tr I II Hn I II Tb	K
386	(arr. Knight)	Handel for Brass	Tr I II Tb I (Hn) II	KPM
387		Sonatas in F and A	Tr Pf	UMP
388		Largo	Hn Pf	UMP
389		Concerto in F minor	Tb Pf	BH/ UMP
390		Concerto in G minor	Tr Pf	Univ
391		Chaconne (*Almira*)	Tr I II Tb Tba	Sch
392	Harris, A.	Theme and Variations	Hn I II III IV V VI VII VIII	K
393	Hartel, J. W.	Concerto no. 2 E♭	Tr Pf	MR
394	Harvey, P.	Graded Study Duets	Tr I II (Hn I II)	BH
395	Hasquenoph, P.	Divertissement	Tr I II III Hn I II III Tb I II III Tba (optional Perc)	Univ
396	Haussmann	Three Dances	Tr I II Tb I II III	BR
397	Haydn, J.	Concerto No. 1	Hn Pf	BH
398		Concerto No. 2	Hn Pf	BH
399		Minuet from Op. 76 No. 3	Tr I II Tb I (Hn) II	K
400		A Haydn Solo Album	Tr Pf	OUP
401		Trumpet Concerto E♭	Tr Pf	U/Sch/B/ BH

	Composer	*Title*	*Instruments*	*Publisher*
402		Horn Concerto No. 1	Hn Pf	B/BH
403		Horn Concerto No. 2	Hn Pf	B/BH
404	Haydn, M.	Concerto in D	Hn Pf	H
405	Heisz, H.	Trumpet Music (1934)	Tr I II (in C) Tb I II	BR
406	Hess	Sonatina	Tr Pf	H
407	Hindemith, P.	Morning Music from 'Plöner Musiktag'	Tr I II Tb I II (Tba)	BH
408		Concerto	Hn Pf	S
409		Sonata	Tb Pf	S
410		Sonata	Hn Pf	S
411		Sonata	Tba Pf	S
412		Sonata	Tr Pf	S
413		Sonata	Hn I II III IV	S
414	Hoddinott, A.	Rondo Scherzo	Tr Pf	OUP
415		Sonata	Hn Pf	OUP
416	Holborne, A. (arr. Dart)	Suite	Tr I II Tb I II III or Tr I II Hn (E♭) Tb Euph	OUP
417		Pavans, Galliards, Almains, etc. (1599)	Tr I II (Hn) Tb I (Hn) II III (Bar)	K
418		Five-Part Brass Music	Tr I II Tb I II III	MR
419		Complete Brass Music vols. 1 and 2	Tr I II Tb I (Hn) II III	MR
420	Honegger, A.	Intrada	Tr Pf	UMP
421	Horovitz, J.	Music Hall Suite	Tr I II Hn Tb Tba	N
422		Trumpet Concerto	Tr Pf	N
423		Adam-Blues	Tb Pf	N
424		Euphonium Concerto	Euph Pf	N
425	Horson, H.	Suite for Brass No. 2	Tr I II Hn Tb	S
426	Höser, O.	Romanze	Tb Pf	L
427	Hovhaness, A.	Canzona and Fugue Op. 72	Tr I II Hn Tb (Tba)	H
428		Six Dances Op. 79	Tr I II Hn Tb Tba	H
429		'Artik' Concerto	Hn Pf	H
430		Resurrection, Aria, and Fugue	Tr Pf	H
431		Khaldis	Tr I II III IV Pf Perc	K
432		Sharagan and Fugue	Tr I II Tb I (Hn) II	K
433		Fantasy Op. 70 No. 1	Tr Hn Tb	H

	Composer	*Title*	*Instruments*	*Publisher*
434		Fantasy Op. 70 No. 2	Tr Hn Tb	H
435		Fantasy Op. 70 No. 3	Tr Hn Tb	H
436		Fantasy Op. 70 No. 4	Tr I II Hn Tb (Tba)	H
437		Fantasy Op. 70 No. 5	Tr I II Hn Tb (Tba)	H
438	Howe (arr.)	Three Madrigals (Gibbons, Byrd, Morley)	Tr I II Hn Tb Bar Tba	UMP
439	Hummel, J.	Trumpet Concerto	Tr Pf	K
440		Trumpet Concerto	Tr Pf	BH/ Univ
441		Trumpet Concerto	Tr Pf	UMP
442	Ibert, J.	Impromptu	Tr Pf	UMP
443	Isaac, H.	Three Isaac Pieces	Tr Hn Tb	E
444	Jacob, G.	Concerto for Horn	Hn Pf	SB
445		Concerto for Trombone	Tb Pf	SB
446		Scherzo	Tr I II Hn Tb	SB
447		Tuba Suite	Tba Pf	BH
448		Suite	Tb I II III IV	BH
449	Jelich	Ricercare	Tr Tb	B
450	Johnson, S.	An Intermediate Horn Book	Hn Pf	OUP
451	Jolivet, A.	Second Trumpet Concerto	Tr Pf	UMP
452		Fanfare	Ensemble	UMP
453		Arioso barocco	Tr Organ	UMP
454		Concertino	Tr Pf	UMP
455	Jørgensen, A.	Suite	Tb Pf	C
456	Josquin des Prés	Motet and Royal Fanfare	Tr I II (Hn) Tb I (Hn) II	K
457		Three Josquin Pieces	Tr Hn Tb	E
458	Kalabis	Sonata Op. 32	Tb Pf	S
459	Karg-Elert, S.	Nun danket alle Gott	Tr I II III Pf (Organ)	K
460	Kazdin, A.	Twelve Duos	Tr Hn	K
461	Keller, H.	Quartet	Tr I II Tb I II	K
462	Kelly, B.	Fanfares and Sonatina for Brass Sextet	Tr I II Hn (Tr III) Tb I (Hn) II III	N
463	Kerry, B.	Fanfare and March	Tr I II Hn (in F or E♭) Tb (Euph/ Bar/Tba)	C
464	Kesnar, M.	Intermezzo	Tr I II Hn Tb	Univ

	Composer	Title	Instruments	Publisher
465	Kessel, J.	Sonata	Tr I II Tb (Hn) II III (Tba)	K
466	Kilar, W.	Sonata	Hn Pf	Univ
467	King, R.	Suite française	Tr Bar/Euph (Tb)	K
468		Prelude and Fugue	Tr I II Tb I II (Bar) Organ	K
469	(arr.)	Early German Chorales	Tb I II III IV	K
470	Koch, J. H. E.	Sinfonietta	Tr I II III Tb I II III Timpani	B
471	Kont, P.	Trio	Tr Hn Tb	Univ
472		Quartet	Tr Hn Tb Tba	Univ
473		Quartettino	Tr Hn I II Tb	Univ
474	Korda, V.	Sonatina	Tr Pf	Univ
475	Korn, P. J.	Prelude and Scherzo	Tr I II Hn Tb I II (Tba)	BH
476	Korte, K.	Introductions	Tr I II (B♭ or C) Hn Tb Tba	UMP
477	Kreisler, A.	Music for Brass Quartet	Tr I II Hn Tb	BH
478		Concert piece	Tr I II Hn Tb	BH
479	Kremer	Three Aphorisms (1967)	Tr I II Tb I II	B
480	Křenek, E.	Five Pieces	Tr Pf	B
481	Krol, B.	Little Festival Music	Hn I II III IV	B
482	Kühn, S.	Adagio from Military Concerto	Tb Pf	H
483	Kurz	Concerto	Tr Pf	Br
484	Lamy, F.	Choral varié	Tb Pf	UMP
485	Lang, I.	Concerto bucolico	Hn Pf	B
486	Langley, J. W.	Suite	Tb I II III IV (Tba)	H
487	Langrish, H. (arr.)	Eight Easy Pieces	Hn Pf	OUP
488	Langstroth (arr.)	Five Dances of the 16th and 17th Centuries	Tr I II Tb I II	Univ
489	Lappi, P.	Canzona 'La Negrona' a8	Ensemble (4 Tr 2 Hn 2 Tb) (2 x 4)	H
490		Canzoni 11 and 12	Tr I II II Tb I (Hn) II	MR
491		Canzona 26	Tr I II III IV Tb I (Hn) II III IV	MR

	Composer	Title	Instruments	Publisher
492	Larsson, L.-E.	Concertino Op. 45	Tr Pf	C
493	Lassus, O.	Four Tudor Canzonas	Tr I II Hn (F or E♭) Tb (Euph/ Bass)	C
494		Providebam Dominum	Tr I II III Organ or Tr I II III IV Hn Tb I II (Tba)	K
495	Latham, W.	Suite	Tr Pf	Univ
496	Lawton, S. M. (arr.)	The Young Trombonist vols. 1-3	Tb Pf	OUP
497		The Young Trumpet Player vols. 1-3	Tr Pf	OUP
498		Old English Trumpet Tunes	Tr Pf	OUP
499		The Young Horn Player vols. 1-3	Hn Pf	OUP
500		The Brass Quartet vols. 1 and 2	Tr I II Tb I (Hn) II	OUP
501	Laycock, H.	Solo Album for Trombone	Tb Pf	BH
502	Lefebvre	Romance	Hn Pf	UMP
503	Lehner, F. X.	Sonatina	Tb Pf	B
504	Lessard, J.	Quodlibets	Tr I II Tb	N
505	Lethbridge, L.	Eight Solos for Horn in F	Hn Pf	OUP
		The Brass Quartet Vols. 3 and 4		
506	Lewis, A.	Concerto for Horn	Hn Pf	L
507		Concerto for Trumpet	Tr Pf	L
508	Lloyd Webber	Suite in F	Tr Pf	E
509	Locke, M.	Music for His Majesty's Sackbuts and Cornetts (1661)	Tr I II Hn Tb I II III	OUP
510		Music for King Charles II	Tr I II III Tb I (Hn) II III (Bar)	K
511	Loeillet, J. B.	Sonata in G	Tr Pf	UMP
512	London, P.	The Trombone Serenade	Tb Pf	C
513	Louthe, R.	Concertino	Tr Pf	C
514	Lovelock, W.	Three Pieces for Brass Quartet	Tr I II Hn (F or E♭) Tb (Euph/ Bass)	C

	Composer	Title	Instruments	Publisher
515	Lübeck	Processional Music	Tr I II III IV (optional V) Perc	B
516	Lully, J. B.	Overture *Cadmus et Hermione*	Tr I II Hn Tb I II (Bar)	K
517	Lutyens, E.	Duo Op. 34 No. 1	Hn Pf	S
518	Luzzaschi, L.	Canzona 10	Tr I II Tb I (Hn) II	MR
519	Malige, F.	Quartet	Hn I II III IV	BR
520	Manfredini, F.	Concerto in D	Tr I II Pf	UMP
521	Manzos	Concerto	Tb Pf	H
522	Marcadante	Salve Maria	Tb Pf	H
523	Marcello, B.	The heavens are telling	Tr I II Tb I (Hn) II (Bar) Organ	K
524		The Lord will hear	As above	K
525	Marini, B.	Canzon decima a 6	Tr I II Tb I (Hn) II III (Euph) IV (Tba)	E
526		Canzon ottava a 6	As above	E
527		Canzona	Tb I II III IV	E
528	Marshall, N.	An Album for the Horn	Hn Pf	OUP
529	Martin, F.	Ballade	Tb Pf	Univ
530	Martini, G. B.	Gavotte	Hn Pf	H
531	Marx, K.	Turm-Musik Op. 37 No. 1	Tr I II III Tb I II (optional Perc)	B
532	Maschera, F.	Two Canzonas (Bk. 1 Nos. 5 and 7)	Tr I II Tb I (Hn) II	MR
533		Two Canzonas (Bk. 1 Nos. 13 and 12)	As above	MR
534	Massaino, T.	Canzona (1608) a8	Ensemble (2 × 4)	H
535		Canzona (1608) a8	Tb I II III IV V VI VII VIII	K
536		Canzona 33	Tr I II III IV Tb I (Hn) II III IV	MR
537		Canzon a8	Ensemble (4 Tr 2 Hn 2 Tb)	H
538	Mattheson, J.	Air	Hn Pf	NWM
539	Maurer, L.	Twelve Little Pieces	Tr I II Hn Tb Tba	N
540	Mayer, W.	Quintet	Tr I II Hn Tb Tba	UMP

	Composer	Title	Instruments	Publisher
541	McCabe, J.	Fantasy for Brass Quartet	Tr I II Hn (Tb) Tb	N
542		Rounds for Brass Quintet	Tr (in C) Tr (B♭) Hn Tb Tba	N
543	McCarty, P.	Recitative and Fugue	Tb I II III IV	K
544	McKay, G. F.	Two Pieces	Tr I II Tb I II	Univ
545	McKenna, J. R. and Swinburne, W. H.	Brass for Beginners	Ensemble	OUP
546	Mellers, W.	Galliard	Tb Pf	S
547	Merulo, C.	Canzona 5	Tr I II Tb I (Hn) II	MR
548		Canzonas 18, 23, 36	Tr I II Tb I (Hn) II III	MR
549	Meyer, J.	Moussaillon-Marche	Tr Pf	UMP
550	Mihalovici, M.	Variations	Hn Pf	UMP
551	Milhaud, D.	Concertino d'hiver	Tr Pf	Sch
552	Metra, O.	Danses Célèbres	Tr Pf	UMP
553	Molter	Concertos for 1, 2, & 3 Trumpets	Tr I (optional II III) Pf	MR
554	Monteverdi, C.	Three Sinfonias (*Orfeo*)	Tr I II Tb I (Hn) II (Hn) II IV V (Tba)	F
555		Gloria Concertata	Tb I II III IV (optional Strings)	B
556	Montico, M.	Caccia	Hn Pf	H
557		Elegia	Hn Pf	H
558	Moortel, L. van de	Allegro marziale	Tr Pf	UMP
559	Morley, T.	Now is the month of maying	Tb I II III IV	E
560		My bonnie lass	Tb I II III IV	E
561	Mouret	Symphonies de fanfares	Tr I II III Tb I II III Tba	UMP
562		Two Divertissements	Hn Pf	UMP
563	Mozart, L.	Concerto	Tr Pf	H
564	Mozart W. A.	Divertimento	Tr I II III (optional IV)	BH
565		Adagio from Clarinet Concerto	Hn Pf	H
566		Horn Concerto K447	Hn Pf	H
567		Horn Quintet K407	Hn Pf	H

	Composer	Title	Instruments	Publisher
568		Larghetto from Clarinet Quintet	Hn Pf	H
569		Piano Sonata K322	Hn Pf	H
570		Pantomime from *Les Petits Riens*	Ensemble a4	Univ
571		A Mozart Solo Album	Tr (Tb) Pf	OUP
572		Fugue K401	Tr I II (Hn) Tb I (Hn) II	K
573		Two Themes	Tr I II Tb I (Hn) II	K
574		Horn Concerto No. 1	Hn Pf	S/BR
575		Horn Concerto No. 2	Hn Pf	S/BR
576		Horn Concerto No. 3	Hn Pf	S/BR
577		Horn Concerto No. 4	Hn Pf	S/BR
578		Concerto Rondo E♭	Hn Pf	S/BR/ BH
579		Larghetto	Hn Pf	UMP
580		Quintet E♭ K407	Hn Pf	S
581	Muczynski, R.	Trumpet Trio	Tr I II III	Sch
582		Voyage Op. 27	Tr Hn Tb	Sch
583	Müller–Zürich	Chorale Fantasia	Tr I II Tb I II Organ	B
584		Chorale Toccata	Tr I II Tb I II Organ	B
585	Müller	Quartets (Bks. 1-4)	Mixed Quartet	BH
586		Quartets (Bks. 1-3)	Tb I II III IV	BH
587	Mussorgsky, M.	Capriccio	Tr I II Hn Tb	Univ
588	Nagel, R. (arr.)	Baroque Music for Trumpet	Tr Pf	BH
589		The Regal Trumpet	Tr Pf	BH
590	Nelhybel, V.	Numismata for 7 brass instruments	Tr I II Hn I II Tb I II Tba	N
591		Six Pieces for Four Trombones	Tb I II III IV	N
592		Trio for Brass	Tr Hn Tb	N
593		Designs for Brass	Tr I II III Hn I II III IV Tb I II III Euph Tba	BH
594		Scherzo Concertante	Hn Pf	N
595		Suite	Tr Pf	N
596		Suite	Tba Pf	N

	Composer	Title	Instruments	Publisher
597	Newsome, R.	Two London Sketches	Tr I II Hn Tb Tba	Feld-man
598	Novy, D.	Sonatina	Tr I II III Hn I II III Tb I II III (optional Perc)	K
599	Obrecht, J.	T'saat een meskin	Tr I Tb I (Hn) II III	K
600	Onozo, J. & Kovacs, M.	Horn Music for Beginners	Hn Pf	BH
601	Orlinski, H. B.	Concert Piece	Tb Pf	B
602	Orr, B.	Divertimento (1969)	Tr I II Hn Tb Tba	N
603	Orr, R.	Serenade	Hn Pf	S
604	Osborne, W.	Four Fanfares	Tr I II III (optional Perc)	K
605		Prelude	Tr I II III (Hn) Tb I (Hn) II III	K
606		Two Ricercars	Tr I II Hn I II Tb I II	K
607	Pachelbel, J.	Two Magnificats	Tr I II (Hn) Tb I (Hn) II	K
608		Allein Gott in der Höh' sei Ehr	Tr I II Tb I (Hn) II (Bar) Organ	K
609	Page, C. (arr.)	Eighteen Concert Pieces	Hn Pf	Univ
610	Palestrina, L.	Three Hymns	Tr I II (Hn) Tb I (Hn) II	K
611		Ricercar	Tr I II (Hn) Tb I (Hn) II	K
612	Panufnik, A.	Concerto in Modo Antico	Tr Pf	BH
613	Patterson, P.	Trumpet Concerto	Tr Pf	W
614		Horn Concerto	Hn Pf	W
615	Peeters, F.	Sonata	Tr Pf	H
616		Suite Op. 82	Tb I II III IV	H
617	Pergolesi, G. B.	Siciliana	Hn Pf	UMP
618	Persichetti, V.	Parable	Tr I II (in C) Hn Tb Tba	UMP UMP
619	Perilhon, A.	Chasse	Hn I II III IV	UMP
620	Pezel, J.	Wind Music a5 Nos. 13, 63, 62	Tr I II Tb I (Hn) II III (Bar)	K
621		Wind Music a5 Nos. 59, 25, 36, 29, 30, 64	Tr I II Tb I (Hn) Tb II III (Bar)	K

	Composer	Title	Instruments	Publisher
622		Hora Decima Nos. 1, 2, 3	Tr I II Tb I (Hn) II III (Tba)	K
623		Hora Decima No. 22	Tr I II Tb I (Hn) II III (Tba)	K
624		Hora Decima No. 25	Tr I II Tb I (Hn) II III (Tba)	K
625		Turmmusik (Tower Music) 18 Pieces	Tr I II Tb I II III	BR
626		Hora Decima: Tower Sonata	Tr I II Tb I II III	BR
627		5-part Brass Music vols. 1-3	Tr I II Tb I(Hn)II III	MR
628		Hora Decima vols. 1, 2	Tr I II Tb I(Hn)II III	MR
629		Three Sonatas	Tr I II Pf(Organ)	K
630		Sonata No. 2	Tr I II Tb I(Hn) II(Bar) Organ	K
631		Sonatinas 63-73	Tr I II Pf	MR
632		12 Sonatas	Tr I II Tb I(Hn) II III	E
633		Sixteen Dances	Tr I II Tb I(Hn) II III	E
634	Phillips, B.	Trio	Tr I II III	K
635		Piece	Tb I II III IV V VI	K
636	Phillips, I. C.	A Classical & Romantic Album for the Horn	Hn(in F or E♭) Pf	OUP
637		A Classical & Romantic Album for the Trombone	Tb Pf	OUP
638	(see also Forbes, W.)	A Classical & Romantic Album for the Trumpet	Tr Pf	OUP
639	Pichter	Brass Music	Tr I II Hn I II Tb I II	Univ
640	Pilss, K.	Concerto in B♭	Tr Pf	Univ
641		Sonata	Tr Pf	Univ
642	Pinkham, D.	Trio	Tr Hn Tb	H
643	Poot, M.	Sarabande	Hn Pf	UMP
644	Poulenc, F.	Sonata	Hn Tr Tb	C
645		Elégie	Hn Pf	C

	Composer	Title	Instruments	Publisher
646	Praetorius, M.	In dulci Jubilo	Tr I II Tb I(Hn) II(Bar) Organ	K
647		Two Ancient Carols	Tb I II III IV	E
648	Premru, R.	Tissington Variations	Tb I II III IV	MR
649	Purcell (Clarke)	Trumpet Voluntary	Tr I II(optional III) Tb I(Hn) II III(Tba)	K
650	Purcell, H.	Voluntary on Old Hundredth	Tr I II Tb I(Hn) II III(Tba)	K
651		Symphony from Mvt. 4 of *The Fairy Queen*	Tr I II III IV Hn I II Tb I II III IV (optional Perc)	K
652		The Queen's Dolour	Tr Pf	UMP
653		March & Canzona for the Funeral of Queen Mary	Tr I II Tb I II(optional Perc)	OUP
654		A Purcell Suite	Tr I II(optional III or Hn) Tb I II	OUP
655		Sonata	Tr Pf(Organ)	K
656		Allegro and Air from *King Arthur*	Tr I II Tb I(Hn) II	K
657		Music for Queen Mary	Tr I II(Hn) Tb I(Hn) II	K
658		Two Trumpet Tunes & Ayre	Tr I II Tb I(Hn) II	K
659		Trumpet Tune	Tr I II III Tb I II III Tba	UMP
660		Suite	Tr Pf(Organ)	UMP
661		A Purcell & Handel Album for 2 Trumpets	Tr I II Pf	OUP
662		Overture *Indian Queen*	Tr Pf	MR
663		Overture *Fairy Queen*	Tr I II Pf	MR
664		Overture *St Cecilia's Day*	Tr I II Pf	MR
665		Sonatas I & II	Tr Pf	MR
666	Ramsey, H.	A Celtic Lament	Hn Pf	H
667	Ramsoe, W.	Quartet No. 5	Tr I II Hn(Tb) Bar(Tb)	K
668		Quartets 1 & 2	Tr I II Tb I II(Tba)	E
669	Rasmussen, M.	Christmas Music (40 Carols)	Tr I II Tb I(Hn) II	K

	Composer	*Title*	*Instruments*	*Publisher*
670	Ratez	Reveil	Tr Pf	UMP
671	Ravel, M.	Pavane	Tr Pf	Univ
672	Read, G.	De profundis	Hn/Tb Pf(Organ)	K
673	Reder, P.	Five American Marches	Tr I II (Hn I II or Tb I II) Perc	N
674		Five French Marches	Tr I II (Hn I II or Tb I II) Perc	N
675		Five Parade Ground Marches	As above	N
676		Four Tattoos & A Night Piece	As above	N
677	Reger, M.	Romance in G	Hn (Tr) Pf	BR
678	Reiche, G.	Six Trios Op. 82	Hn I II III	BH
679		Sonata No. 1	Tr I II(Hn) Tb I(Hn) II	K
680		Sonata No. 7	As above	K
681		Sonata No. 15	As above	K
682		Sonata No. 18	As above	K
683		Sonata No. 19	As above	K
684		Two Sonatas 21, 22	As above	K
685		Sonata 24	As above	K
686		24 New Quatricinia	Tr Tb I(Hn/Tr) II III	E
687	Reiter, A.	Music for Brass	Tr I II III Hn I II(E♭ Hn) Tb I II Tba	Univ
688		Music for Brass	Tb(Solo) Hn I II III E♭ Hn I II III IV V	Univ
689		Music for Brass	Tr(Solo) Hn I II III E♭ Hn I II Tba	Univ
690		Sonatina	Hn Pf	Univ
691	Reynolds, V.	Music for Five Trumpets	Tr I II III IV V	K
692		Short Suite	Hn I II III IV	K
693	Richardson, N. (arr.)	Six Trumpet Tunes	Tr Pf	BH
694		Six More Trumpet Tunes	Tr Pf	BH
695		Six Horn Tunes	Hn Pf	BH
696	Riisager, K.	Concertino	Tr Pf	C
697	Rimsky-Korsakov	Two Duets	Tr I II (Hn I II)	K

	Composer	Title	Instruments	Publisher
698		Notturno	Hn I II III IV (Tr I II Tb I II)	K
699		Concerto	Tb Pf	BH
700	Rivier, J.	Concerto	Tr Pf	UMP
701	Rivers, P. (arr.)	Folk Tunes for Brass	Any quintet	KPM
702	Roger, K. G.	Concerto Grosso	Tr Pf	C
703	Rognoni-Taeggio, G.	Canzona 'La Porta' a 8	Ensemble (2 x 4)	H
704	Roikjer, K.	Variations & Fugue	Tr I II(Tb or Tba)	C
705		Scherzo Op. 58	Tr I II(Hn, Tb, or Tba)	C
706	Roper, K.	Triptych	Hn Pf	T
707	Rosenmüller, J.	Eleven Sonate de Camera (1670)	Tr I II Tb I II	Univ
708	Ross, W.	Concerto	Tb Pf	BH
709		Concerto for Brass Quintet & Orchestra	Tr I II Hn Tb Tba Pf	BH
710	Rossi, S.	Sinfonie, gagliarde, canzone 1607-1608	Tr I II Hn(Tb) Tb	E
711		Sinfonie, gagliarde 1607-1608	Tr I II Tb(Hn) II(Hn) III	E
712	Rossini, G.	Prelude, Theme, and Variations (1857)	Hn (in F or E♭) Pf	H
713	Roy, K. G.	Sonata	Tb Pf	K
714	Rubbra, E.	Fanfare for Europe	Tr I II III IV V VI (in C)	L
715	Rueff, J.	Two Short Pieces	Tb I II III IV	UMP
716	Ruyssen, P.	Allegro	Tr Pf	SB
717	Sachse, H. W.	Sonata	Hn Pf	H
718	Saint-Saëns, C.	Romance Op. 67	Hn Pf	UMP
719		Morceau de concert Op. 94	Hn Pf	UMP
720		Cavatine	Tb Pf	UMP
721	Samuel—Rousseau	Piece Concertante	Tb Pf	UMP
722	Sanders, R.	Sonata in B flat	Hn Pf	OUP
723		Suite	Tr I II Tb I II	K
724		Square Dance	Tr Pf	SB
725	Scarlatti, A.	Sinfonia	Tr Pf	MR
726		Two Sinfonias	Tr I II Pf	MR
727	Schafer, K.	Sonatina	Tr Pf	B
728		Nine Pieces (1959)	Tr I II	B
729		Five Pieces	Tr I II III	B

	Composer	Title	Instruments	Publisher
730	Scheidt, S.	Suite	Tr I II Hn Tb Tba	Univ
731		Canzona	Tr I II III IV(Hn I II III IV)	K
732		Da Jesus an dem Kreuze	Tb I(Hn) II III IV(Tba)	K
733		Three Christmas Chorales	Tr I II(Hn) Tb I(Hn) II(Bar)	K
734		Spielmusik (5 pieces)	Tr I II Tb I II	B
735		Suite in C	Tr I II Tb I II	B
736		Canzon (1621)	Tr I II III IV	K
737		Canzona Bergamesca	Tr I II Hn Tb Tba	E
738	Schein, J.	Two Pieces	Tr I II Tb I(Hn) II(Hn) III	K
739	Scheurer, R.	Scherzo	Tr I II Hn I II Tb I II Perc	Univ
740	Schicht (arr. Surtes)	Great is the Lord	Tr I II Tb I II (Hn, Euph, or Bar)	CH
741	Schiffman	Holiday Fanfares	Tr I II III(Hn I II III)	K
742	Schickele, P.	Monochrome II	Tb I II III IV V VI VII	UMP
743	Schilling, H.	Canzona (1966)	Tr Pf	BR
744		Musica Festiva I & II	Tr I II Tb I II(optional Perc)	BR
745		Fanfare, Ricercare, and Hymn	Tr I II III(in C) Tb I II III	BR
746		Intrada	Tr I II III(in B♭) Tb I II III	BR
747		Tripartita	Tr I II Hn Tb Tba(optional Perc)	UMP
748	Schiske, K.	Trumpet Music Op. 13	Tr I-X Tb I-VIII Tba I II(optional Perc)	Univ
749	Schmitt, F.	Fanfare *Antony and Cleopatra*	Tr I II III Hn I II III IV Tb I II III Tba Perc	UMP
750		Tower Music	Tr I II III IV V VI (optional Perc)	BR
751		Koenigsfanfaren	Tr I II III IV V VI Hn I II III IV Tb I II III Tba Timpani	W

	Composer	Title	Instruments	Publisher
752	Schneider, W.	Little Pieces by Old Masters	Tr Pf	S
753		Classical Pieces	Tr I II(Hn I II)	B
754	Schoeck, O.	Concerto Op. 65	Hn Pf	BH
755	Schollum	Suite	Tr Pf	B
756	Schroder, W.	Andante cantabile	Tb Pf	C
757	Schubert, F.	Ave Maria	Tr Pf	BH
758		Adagio from 'Arpeggione' Sonata	Hn Pf	H
759		Shepherd Melody from *Rosamunde*	Tr I II Hn Tb Tba	Univ
760		Eine kleine Trauer-musik	Tr I II Hn I II Tb I II III(Bar)	K
761		Serenade	Hn Pf	UMP
762	Schumann, R.	Robert Schumann Album	Hn Pf	Sch
763		Adagio & Allegro Op. 70	Hn Pf	BR/H/ BH
764		Konzertstück Op. 86	Hn Pf	BR
765		Abendlied & Träumerei	Tb Pf	H
766	Schütz, H. (arr. Anthony)	Antiphony No. 1 (Motet)	Tr I II III IV Tb I II III IV	Univ
767	Schwaen	Three Ostinati	Tr Pf	H
768	Searle, H.	Aubade	Hn Pf	S
769	Seiber, M.	Notturno	Hn Pf	S
770	Senaillé, J. B.	Introduction & Allegro Spiritoso	Tb(Tba) Pf	H
771	Serocki, K.	Suite	Tb I II III IV	Univ
772		Concerto	Tb Pf	Univ
773		Sonatina	Tb Pf	Univ
774	Siebert, E. (arr.)	Junior Album for Brass Quartet	Any mixed quartet	BH
775		Latin-American Album	Tr I(optional II) Pf	BH
776		Bees-a-Buzzin'	Tr I II Tb I II(Bar)	K
777	Sikorski, K.	Concerto	Hn Pf	Univ
778	Simpson, T.	Pavans, Galliards, Intradas, and Canzonas (1617)	Tr I II Tb I II III	MR
779	Simpson, R.	Canzona a8	Tr I II III IV Tb I II III Tba	L

	Composer	Title	Instruments	Publisher
780	Skorzeny	Concerto	Tr Pf	Univ
781	Smith, D.	Theme and Variations	Tr Hn Tb	T
782	Smith, E. (arr.)	Hymn Tunes for Brass	Any quartet	KPM
783	Snyder, R.	Ricercare	Hn I II III IV	K
784	Soltzer, T.	Fantasia	Tb I II III IV	K
785	Speer, D.	Two Sonatas	Tr I II(Tb) Tb I II	E
786		Two Sonatas	Tr I II Tb I(Hn) II III	E
787		Sonata	Tb I II III IV	E
788	Sperger, J.	Jagdmusik (Hunting Music)	Hn I II	S
789	Stanley, J.	Concerto	Tr Pf	Univ
790		Trumpet Tune	Tr Pf	OUP
791	Starer, R.	Dirge	Tr I II Tb I II	Univ
792	Stephenson, R.	Intradas	Tr I II Tb I(Hn) II	CH
793	Stevens, H.	Sonata	Tr Pf	H
794		Sonata	Hn Pf	K
795	Stoerl, J. G. C.	Six Sonatas	Tr I Tb I(Hn/Tr) Tb II III	E
796	Stoelzel, G. H.	Concerto in D Major	Tr Pf	UMP
797	Stoker, R.	Litany, Sequence, and Hymn	Tr I II Hn Tb	H
798		Festival Suite	Tr Pf	CH
799	Stoltzer, T.	Fantasia	Tr I II Tb I II III(Tba)	K
800	Stone, D. (arr.)	The Minstrel's Gallery	Tr I II Hn(in F or E♭)	BH
801	Stradella, A.	Sinfonia 'Il Barcheggio'	Tr Pf	MR
802	Stravinsky, I.	Fanfare for a New Theatre	Tr I II	BH
803	Süssmuth, R.	Suite	Hn I II III IV	BR
804	Strauss, F.	Introduction, Theme, & Variations	Hn Pf	N
805	Strauss, R.	Concerto No. 1 in E♭ (Op. 11)	Hn Pf	Univ
806		Concerto No. 2 in E♭	Hn Pf	Univ/ BH
807	Sweelinck, J. P.	Rîmes françoises et italiennes (1612)	Tr I II	B
808	Szelenyi, I.	Suite	Tr I II Tb I II	S
809	Takacs, J.	Sonata Breve	Tr Pf	Univ
810	Tartini, G.	Largo and Allegro	Tr Pf	Univ

	Composer	Title	Instruments	Publisher
811	Taverner, J.	Audivi	Tb I II III IV	E
812	Taylor, E.	Chorale, Ground, & March	Tr Pf	H
813	Tchaikowsky, P.	Chanson Triste Op. 40	Hn Pf	BH
814		The Hunt	Tr I II Hn Tb	Univ
815		Humoresque	Tr I II Hn Tb	Univ
816	Tcherepnin, A.	Fanfare	Ensemble	BH
817		March	Tr I II III	BH
818		Trio	Tr I II III	BH
819		Andante	Tb Pf	H
820	Telemann, G. P.	Concerto in D	Hn Pf	H
821		Air	Tr Pf	H
822		Two Concertos	Tr I II III Pf	MR
823		Concerto in C minor	Tr I II Pf	UMP
824		Three Suites	Tr Pf	MR
825		Concerto in B♭	Tr Pf	UMP
826		Two Concertos	Tr Pf	MR
827		Heroic Music	Tr Hn Tb Pf	OUP
828		Sinfonia	Tr Pf	MR
829		Sonata in A minor	Tb Pf	Univ
830	(arr. Lumsden)	Concerto a4	Tb I II III IV	MR
831		Concerto	Tr I II Pf	Univ
832		Twelve Heroic Marches	Tr Pf	UMP
833	Tessarini	Sonata in D major	Tr Pf	UMP
834	Tippett, M.	Sonata for Four Horns	Hn I II III IV	S
835		Fanfare No. 1	Tr I II III Hn I II III IV Tb I II III	S
836		Fanfare No. 2	Tr I II III IV	S
837		Fanfare No. 3	Tr I II III	S
838	Tomasi, H.	To be or not to be	Tb I II III IV(Tba)	UMP
839		Cinq Danses profanes et sacrées	Tba Pf	UMP
840		Petite Suite	Hn I II III IV	UMP
841		Suite	Tr I II III	UMP
842	Tomkins, T.	Mr. Curch's Toye	Tr I II Hn(in F or E♭) Tb(Euph/Bar)	CH
843	Torelli, G.	Concerto in D major	Tr Pf	UMP
844		Six Sonatas	Tr Pf	MR
845		Nine Sinfonias	Tr Pf	MR
846		Two Sonatas	Tr I II Pf	MR
847		Eight Sinfonias	Tr I II Pf	MR
848		Six Concertos	Tr I II Pf	MR

	Composer	Title	Instruments	Publisher
849		Sinfonia con Tromba	Tr Pf(Organ)	K
850		Concerto in C	Tr I II Pf	Univ
851		Concerto in D	Tr Pf	Univ/ UMP
852		Concerto in C	Tr Pf	Univ
853	Traulsen, P.	Trombone Humoresque	Tb Pf	C
854	Turok, P.	Elegy Op. 23	Tr I II III Hn I II Tb I II III Bar Tba	MR
855	Tuthill, B.	Concerto	Tb Pf	K
856	Ulrich, J.	5 Duets for Brass	Tr I II(Hn I II)	C
857	Valentine, R.	18 Easy Pieces	Tr I II	S
858		Sonata in D minor	Tr Pf	UMP
859		Sonata in D major	Tr Pf	UMP
860		Sonata in F major	Tr Pf	UMP
861	Van Doren	Fantasy Concertante	Tr Pf	H
862	Vaughan Williams, R.	Concerto	Tba Pf	OUP
863	Vecchi, O.	Cricket	Tr I II III IV(Hn I II III IV)	G
864	Veracini, F.	Concerto in E minor	Tr Pf	UMP
865	Verrall, J.	Suite	Tr I II Hn Tb I II Tba	Univ
866	Viadana, L.	Sinfonia 'La Bergamasca'	Tr I II III IV Tb I(Hn) II(Hn) III IV	MR
867		Sinfonia 'La Padovana'	As above	MR
868	Villa-Lobos, H.	Preludio from *Bachianas Brasilieras* No. 1	Tb I-VIII	S
869	Vinter, G.	Hunter's Moon	Hn Pf	BH
870	Vitali, G. B.	Capriccioso	Tr I II Hn Euph Tb I II Tba	Univ
871	Vivaldi, A.	Concerto in E♭	Tr I II(in B♭ or C) Pf	Univ
872		Concerto in G minor	Tr Pf	UMP
873		Concerto in F Op. 47 No. 5	Hn I II Pf	R
874		Concerto in C	Tr I II Pf	BH/R/ UMP/ Univ

	Composer	Title	Instruments	Publisher
875		Allegro (from *Juditha*)	Tr Pf	BH/R/ UMP/ Univ
876	Vogel, E.	Music for Brass	Tr I II Hn I II III IV Tb I II III Tba(optional Perc)	Univ
877	Voxman (arr.)	Brass Quartets Vol. 1	Tr I II E♭Hn Tb(Bar)	Rubank (N)
878		Brass Quartets Vol. 2	Tr I II Tb I II(Bar)	Rubank (N)
879	Wagenseil, G. C.	Concerto	Tb Pf	Univ
880	Wagner, R.	Excerpts from Wagner	E♭Hn Tb I II III IV	BH
881		Choral from *Mastersingers*	Ensemble	Univ
882		Pilgrims' Chorus (*Tannhäuser*)	Tb Pf	H
883		Introduction to Act 3 of *Mastersingers*	Tr I II Hn Tb I II III IV(Bar) Tba	K
884		Funeral March from *Götterdämmerung*	Tr I II III Hn I II Tb I II III IV(Bar) Tba	K
885		Introduction and Chorale from *Mastersingers*	Ensemble	BH
886	Walton, W.	A Queen's Fanfare	Tr(E♭) Tr I-VII Tb I II III IV	OUP
887		Fanfare (*Hamlet*)	Tr I II III Hn I II III IV Tb I II III Tba Perc	OUP
888	(arr. de Jongh)	Six Pieces	Tr I II(optional III(Hn)) Tb I II III	OUP
889	Watson, W.	Music for Organ & Horns	Hn I II III IV Organ	Sch
890	Weber, B.	Quartets Nos. 1 & 2	Hn I II III IV	BR
891	Weber, C. M.	Concertino from *Freischütz*	Hn Pf	H
892		Concertino Op. 45	Hn Pf	H
893		Recitative & Prayer from *Freischütz*	Hn Pf	H

	Composer	Title	Instruments	Publisher
894		Adagio from Clarinet Concerto No. 1	Hn Pf	H
895		Concertino Op. 45	Hn Pf	BR
896	Weeks, C.	Triptych	Tb Pf	K
897	Weeks, J.	Jubilate	Tr I II III Hn I II III Tb I II Organ	H
898	Werner, F.	Suite Concertante	Tr Pf	UMP
899	Westcott, F.	Prelude, Pavane, & Galliard	Ensemble 3-part	H
900		Suite	Ensemble 4-part	H
901	White, D. H.	Sonata	Tr Pf	K
902	Widor, C. M.	Salvum fac populum tuum	Tr I II III Tb I II III Tba Organ	UMP
903	Wieschendorff	Theme with Variations	Tba Pf	H
904	Wiggins, B.	First Tunes and Studies for the Trumpet	Tr	OUP
905		First Tunes and Studies for the Trombone or Euphonium	Tb (Euph)	OUP
906	Wildgans, F.	Sonatina (1927)	Hn Pf	Univ
907	Wilkenschildt, G.	Bagatelle	Tr Pf	C
908		Caprice	Tb Pf	C
909		Impromptu	Tb Pf	C
910	Willner, A. (arr.)	Classical Album	Tr Pf	BH
911		Classical Album	Hn Pf	BH
912		Classical Album	Tb Pf	BH
913	Winter, P.	Ceremonial Fanfare	Tr(in C)I II III Tb I II III Tba Perc	H
914	Wolf, de	Andantino	Tr Pf	H
915	Woollen, R.	Triptych	Tr I II III IV Hn I II Tb I II III Tba	H
916	Wright, D.	Music for Brass Ensembles Book 1	Ensemble 4-part	N
917		As above Book 2	Ensemble 4-part	N
918		As above Book 3	Ensemble 4-part	N
919	Wurz	Tower Music I & II	Tr I II III IV Tb I II III IV	BR
920		Tower Music III & IV	Tr I II III Tb I II III	BR

	Composer	Title	Instruments	Publisher
921	Zbinden, J.	Präludium Op. 39	Tr Pf	BR
922		Three Pieces Op. 20	Hn I II III IV	BR
923	Zindars, E.	Quintet	Tr I II Hn Tb Tba	K
924		The Brass Square	Tr I II III IV Hn I II III IV Tb I II III Tba Perc	K
925	Zipp, F.	Three Fanfares	Tr I II III Tb I II III(optional Perc)	H

Guide to catalogue entries for the more common groupings

Trumpet and piano
9 13 14 15 16 17 25 36 37 38 47 52 76 79 80 81 99 100 110
128 131 132 133 136 144 159 160 168 187 188 197 200 204
225 232 235 243 253 255 256 257 259 260 264 265 269 270
337 339 345 346 350 360 370 371 375 378 379 380 381 387
390 393 400 401 406 412 414 420 422 430 439 440 441 442
453 454 474 480 483 492 495 497 498 507 508 511 513 549
558 563 571 588 589 595 612 613 615 638 640 641 652 655
660 662 665 670 671 693 694 696 700 702 716 724 725 727
752 755 757 767 775 780 789 790 793 796 798 801 809 810
812 821 824 825 826 828 832 833 843 844 845 849 851 852
858 859 860 861 864 872 875 898 901 907 910 914 921

2 trumpets (without piano)
20 93 172 250 254 334 697 728 753 802 807 856 857

2 trumpets with piano
38 106 150 520 553 631 661 663 664 726 775 846 847 848 850
871 874

3 trumpets (without piano)
2 20 48 105 220 234 546 581 604 634 729 841

3 trumpets with piano
61 62 219 459 822 831

4 trumpets (without piano)
73 123 151 515 736

Horn and piano
1 3 26 40 45 46 53 74 78 90 97 102 103 109 130 140 143 145
146 152 153 163 165 166 169 170 174 180 183 184 201 207
217 218 222 236 242 245 247 248 283 336 347 351 352 355
373 374 388 397 398 402 403 404 408 410 415 429 444 466
485 487 499 502 505 517 528 530 538 550 556 557 562 565
566 567 568 569 574 575 576 577 578 579 580 594 600 609
614 617 636 643 645 666 672 677 695 706 712 717 718 719
722 754 758 761 762 763 764 768 769 777 794 804 805 806
813 820 869 891 892 893 894 895 906 911

Four horns
32 35 139 181 182 241 413 481 519 619 692 698 731 783 803
834 863 890 922

Trombone with piano
17 24 29 91 125 138 154 196 212 222 230 231 233 330 331
333 349 354 359 365 389 409 423 426 458 482 484 496 501
503 512 521 522 529 546 601 637 699 708 713 720 721 756
765 772 773 853 855 879 882 896 908 909 912

Four trombones
27 31 63 84 85 92 104 134 137 192 240 244 344 448 527 543
559 560 586 616 647 648 715 732 771 787 811 830 838

Mixed quartets
10 18 33 54 55 56 58 59 60 70 71 72 75 82 88 101 108 112
115 126 127 157 161 162 164 173 175 178 186 203 208 209
210 214 249 251 266 277 278 282 284 285 302 303 304 305
332 338 342 357 363 364 368 377 382 383 386 391 399 405
407 427 432 436 437 446 456 463 464 472 473 477 478 479
488 490 493 500 514 518 532 537 541 544 545 547 570 572
573 585 587 607 610 611 653 654 656 657 658 667 668 669
679 680 681 682 683 684 685 686 704 707 710 723 732 733
734 735 740 744 774 776 782 785 791 792 797 800 808 814
815 842 877 878 900 916 917 918

Mixed quintets
11 12 28 34 39 67 69 96 114 141 142 147 156 167 190 194
198 199 228 239 252 267 275 279 308 348 361 369 372 384
396 416 417 418 419 421 428 465 475 476 516 531 539 540
542 548 597 618 620 621 622 623 624 625 626 627 628 632
633 649 650 701 705 711 730 737 738 747 759 778 795 799
880 888 923

Mixed sextets
98 119 205 216 221 226 262 273 274 309 310 311 335 340 385
438 462 510 525 526 605 606 639 739 745 746 865 920 925

Mixed septets
57 68 122 155 237 272 312 313 314 494 554 561 590 659 760
870 913

Mixed octets
5 89 213 280 286 287 288 289 290 291 306 307 315 316 317
318 319 320 328 329 356 358 362 366 489 534 535 536 537
703 766 779 866 868 883 919

Bibliography

Arnold, D., 'Brass instruments in the Italian Church music of the 16th and early 17th centuries', *Brass Quarterly* (1957), pp. 81ff.

Arnold, D., 'Con ogni sorte di stromenti: some practical suggestions', *Brass Quarterly* II (1959), pp. 99ff.

Bate, P., *The trumpet and trombone: an outline of their history, development and construction*, 2nd ed., Benn, 1972

Bach, V., 'Mouthpieces: how to choose a brass instrument mouthpiece', *The Instrumentalist* 26 (Jan. 1972), pp. 32—4

Brand, V., 'British brass bands — amateur music with a professional touch', *The Instrumentalist* 26 (1972), pp. 18—21

Butterworth, A., 'The Brass Band — a cloth-cap joke?', *Music in Education* 34 (1970), pp. 78—9 & 152—3

Caisley, L., 'Brass bands in school', *Sounding Brass* I (Apr. 1972), p. 23

Corley, R., *Brass players' guide to the literature*, Robert King, 1972

D'Ath, N. W., 'The art of practising: Brass', *Music in Education* 36 (1972), pp. 298—9

Dale, D., *Trumpet technique*, Oxford University Press, 1965

Emerson, J., *Music for Woodwind and Brass*, Emerson, 1974

Farkas, P., *The Art of French Horn Playing*, Birchard, 1965

Farkas, P., *The Art of Brass Playing*, Brass Publications, 1956

Fitzpatrick, H., *The horn and horn playing, and the Austro-Bohemian tradition from 1680 to 1830*, Oxford University Press, 1970

Fletcher, J., 'Thoughts on the tuba', *Composer* 44 (1972), pp. 5—12

Fletcher, J., 'Tuba talk', *Sounding Brass* 2 ii (July 1973), pp. 59—61

Fletcher, J., 'More tuba talk', *Sounding Brass* 2 iii (Oct. 1973), pp. 78—9

Fletcher, J., 'Even more tuba talk', *Sounding Brass*, 2 iv (Jan. 1974), pp. 110—12

Fromme, A., 'Performance technique on brass instruments during the seventeenth century', *Journal of research in Music Education* 20 (1972), pp. 329—43

Gregory, R., *The Horn: comprehensive guide to the modern instrument and its music*, Faber, 1961

Gregory, R., *The trombone: the instrument and its music*, Faber, 1973

Hunt, N. J., *A study of the use of baroque ensemble literature in instrumental music-teacher education*, University of California Press, Berkeley, 1966

Kenton, E. F., 'The "brass" parts in Giovanni Gabrieli's instrumental ensemble compositions', *Brass Quarterly* I (1958), pp. 73ff.

Kenton, E. F., *Life and works of Giovanni Gabrieli*, American Institute of Musicology, Rome, 1967

Kleinhammer, E., *The art of trombone playing*, Birchard, 1963

Maxted, G., *Talking about the trombone*, Baker, 1970

McGavin, E. A., *Brass and woodwind: a guide to the purchase and care of musical instruments*, Schools Music Association, 1965

Morley-Pegge, R., *The French horn*, Benn, 1960

Oneglia, M. F., 'The perfect trumpet lesson', *The Instrumentalist* 28 ix (Apr. 1974), pp. 74–7

Periodicals: *Brass Band News* (Monthly)
Brass and Woodwind Quarterly, ed. M. H. Rasmussen, from 1966 (formerly *Brass Quarterly*, Vols. 1–7, 1957–1964); publication irregular
Sounding Brass (and the Conductor), ed. Bram Gay and Edward Gregson, Novello (quarterly from April 1972)
Music in Education, Novello (bi-monthly)

Rasmussen, M., 'On the modern performance of parts originally written for the cornett', *Brass Quarterly* I (1958), pp. 20ff.

Rasmussen, M., *A teacher's guide to the literature of brass instruments*, Appleyard Publications, 2nd ed. 1968

Schuller, G., *Horn technique*, Oxford University Press, 1962

Shoemaker, J. R., 'Brass in Venice', *The Instrumentalist* 27 (1973), pp. 32–3

Smithers, D. L., *The music and history of the baroque trumpet before 1721*, Dent, 1973

Swelby, C., 'Music through the band', *Music Teacher* (June, July, August, Sept. & Oct. 1972)

Tuckwell, B., 'Teaching horn players by the gross', *Music in Education* 38 (1974), pp. 218–20.

Wick, D., *Trombone technique*, Oxford University Press, 1971

Wright, D., *Scoring for Brass Band*, Baker, 4th ed. 1967